Y0-AGK-156

Best College Essays 2014

I plan to live my life by seeing the world from every possible perspective and never allowing reality to limit my imagination.

—Hannah Ades

My name is Ben Aronson. My goal in life is to inspire and help others.

The topics discussed in the essay are ones that I rarely talk about in person, so I felt as if putting them on paper could really help describe them to myself or others. Instead of fretting about my writing style or word choice, I let the thoughts flow onto the page.

—Benjamin Aronson
Attending University of Maryland, College Park

I stared at the screen trying to think of something grand to write. I thought for hours before I realized that the best way to tackle the essay was simply to tell a story.

—Mason Bartle
Attending Brown University

I spent about three brutal, never-ending months on this essay. At first, I wasn't really comfortable writing about myself. Typically, in my English courses, I was taught to write in a flowery manner rather than straightforward and to the point, so it was a strange transition. I learned more and more about myself as I sat down every day picking into the depths of my brain in hopes of discovering "what place/environment makes me content."

—Natalya Brill
Attending Union College

I live in San Diego and my goal in life is to repay my mother by making something out of my life.

—Gerardo Castillo

I live in Brooklyn, New York. I am a city girl who grew up in the Caribbean. My goal is to become a successful individual. I would like to see my name shining somewhere one day. I would like to be a film producer or work in any department in the field of media. My goal is to be happy with whatever I do and become financially stable in life. I would also like to make my family, friends, and hometown proud every step of the way.

—Aria Collins
Attending Ithaca College

I struggled to come up with a topic that I really cared about for this essay, until Ms. Heimer asked me, "What do you want them [the colleges] to know about you?" I responded that I wanted them to know that I have a lot of passion and dedicate a lot of myself to many different hobbies and projects but really want to find one thing to dedicate myself to. That's where the idea for this essay came from, and I think it provides a nice and provocative glimpse into all of the time, energy, and dedication that I have given to my various pursuits thus far in my life.

—Danny Eagan
Attending University of Alaska, Fairbanks

This essay was very hard for me to write because I had to ask my mom many questions, some of which she wasn't comfortable with because it brought back horrible memories.

—Fadumo Farah

My family has helped define the person I am today. It is quirky, interesting, and at times hectic, but my family inspired me to love learning and applying my knowledge to impact the world. I really wanted to write an essay about this, and, after a dozen revisions that attempted to summarize the last eighteen amazing years of time with my family, this final version portrays what I will always take with me.

—Julian Fletcher-Taylor

One day, I was showing my counselor my art portfolio and she pointed to one of the paintings (my self portrait) and she said: "It kind of looks like a cow." I had always thought this portrait looked like a cow, but I stopped telling people this because it seemed too self-critical. However, the more my counselor and I discussed the hilarity of my portrait's appearance, I began to realize that my own perception of my self-portrait was grounded in something much deeper than my literal ability to draw a realistic portrait. Essentially, the unfortunate outcome of this portrait derived from the unique way I viewed the world and, consequently, myself. Because painting has always been an intrinsic part of my personality, I decided to expound upon the perception of my self-portrait and write an essay from there.

—Laura Feigen
Attending Stanford University

I'm a 17-year-old Jewish girl from Chicago, Illinois. My goal in life is to work in diplomacy in an effort to find a peaceful solution for the world's problems.

—Maxine Freedman
Attending Macalester College

My name is Asha Haghi. I am currently living in San Diego, California, but am originally from Kenya. My goals in life include graduating high school, attending a four-year university, and making a living in order to financially assist my single mother.

—Asha Haghi

I attend International School in Bellevue, Washington. I intend on becoming a pediatrician to help realize my passion for serving as a bulwark for immigrant families like mine against the consequences of cultural barriers in the field of medicine.

—Julia Joo

My name is Amanda Lee. Apart from the homework I do every day in my large house-haven in the beautiful land of Colorado, I am a nerd. My life goals include mastering the art of college-ing, staring at penguins, publishing a piece of literature, and solving the diaper-garbage crisis.

—Amanda Lee
Attending Swarthmore College

I interpreted the prompt loosely, and started off with blank verse poetry. I tried embracing an unorthodox college essay to grab the attention of the admissions officers; my essay would be refreshing compared to endless stacks of paragraphs. When I reviewed my essay with my mentor, he said that it was brilliant—but too risky and abstract. So I did what any good student would do, take the abstraction to the extreme! I played with literary devices, tried to sound like my favorite writers, and for the first time, I had fun writing something.

—Kevin Lee

I was playing piano one afternoon, and I realized that my little brother Logan has never failed to dance whenever the piano is playing. All of a sudden, I found myself abruptly getting off the piano bench to find a pen and paper; I started jotting memorable stories about Logan.

—Amanda Lowery
Attending MIT

My school counselor knew I was a really passionate guy who liked to learn and explore but didn't think that was completely visible in my application. He luckily advised me to just tell an honest story that showed I was hungry to learn. I brought it to my counselor and he was excited and said, "This is so you!"

—John McAndrews

One of my goals in life is to facilitate dialogue and bring "enemies" closer together as you will read in this essay.

—Jordon Solomon
Attending Tulane University

My goal is to create a more just world through our US legal system as a civil rights lawyer. I will use my tenacity, commitment and legal training to save the lives particularly of those on the economic and social fringes of American society.

—Tiffany A. Peart
Attending Spelman College

While the essay needed a lot of fine tuning after that initial writing period, the central ideas had taken root. I revised the essay considerably, trying to make it as personal as possible, while also staying concise. Several drafts later, having incorporated some of the suggestions of my brilliant English teacher, I had a finished essay—an essay that carried my voice and reflected my passions in an exciting way.

— Thomas Poston
Attending Wake Forest University

Wow! This was a long journey. I started with a kernel of an idea. I then did a peer review with my English class and they helped me unearth what I was really trying to say. Then I procrastinated for a few weeks and pretended it didn't exist. Then I plunged in. Through writing, and revising, both on my own and with my English teacher, I truly learned a lot about myself—both about my life and about myself as a writer and thinker.

—Ayotunde Summers
Attending University of Buffalo

I live in Nova Scotia, Canada, with my mother, grandmother and younger sister. I hope to someday use art to change the world.

This essay is a patchwork of many different essays I wrote over a period of a few months. Eventually, it came down to selecting the bits that were truest to me and my life and stitching them together.

—Leyla Tonak
Attending Boston University

Best College Essays 2014

Edited and With An Introduction By
Gabrielle Glancy

ONEIRIC
PRESS

Copyright © 2014 by Gabrielle Glancy

All rights reserved. No part of this publication may be reproduced, distributed or transmitted in any form or by any means, including photocopying, recording, or other electronic or mechanical methods, without the prior written permission of the publisher, except in the case of brief quotations embodied in critical reviews and certain other noncommercial uses permitted by copyright law. For permission requests, write to the publisher, addressed "Attention: Permissions Coordinator," at the address below.

Oneiric Press
www.newvisionlearning.org

Book Layout ©2014 BookDesignTemplates.com
Author Photo by Meg Allen
Book Cover by Kit Foster

Best College Essays 2014 / Gabrielle Glancy. —1st ed.
ISBN 978-0-9912149-0-7 (Paperback)
ISBN 978-0-9912149-1-4 (Kindle)
ISBN 978-0-9912149-2-1 (ePub)

Contents

To the college-bound students all across the world who mustered the courage to find their stories, express them in the form of the college essay and submit them to Best College Essays 2014.

To all those who helped these students along the way, including the teachers, parents, and college counselors who told them about Best College Essays *in the first place and who encouraged them to stand up and be counted.*

To the generations of students who are now, or will soon be, face to face with the awesome task of representing themselves in the college essay... May this book be an inspiration and a guide.

Writing my essay was like searching for an obscure jewel that was buried deep inside me. I wanted the essay to show readers the essence of my creative self-expression. To help me "find" the essay, my college guidance counselor held the flashlight while I did the digging! Finally, I struck the roots of my very own family tree, most notably, my grandmother Gwennie, the first woman in our family to go to college and one of the rare African American women in her small upstate, New York town to become a college graduate. The essay I wrote is my personal statement and is also a tribute to my grandmother's bold style and courage that became the inspiration for my essay and have also served to inspire me as a young black woman.

—Chloe Pinkney
Attending Skidmore College

I am not too concerned with what people may think of me, but one thing I cannot stand is the concept of being forgotten. Those who work for the admissions office in any college must read copious amounts of essays. I did not want mine to be just another essay for an admissions counselor to read—I wanted to be remembered.

—Jonathen Munoz
Attending Centenary College of New Jersey

INTRODUCTION

To write an amazing essay, students must take an amazing journey—a journey within—to locate what has moved and formed them, and find a way to put what they discover into words.

This is no easy task, especially because students are asked to write in a form they may never have heard of, let alone mastered—the narrative, personal statement.

The college essay is not like the five-paragraph essay students have been taught to write in school. Nor is it a simple reflection. The fundamental building block of a narrative personal essay is the anecdote. What is an anecdote? A short piece of writing that tells a story. But an anecdote alone does not a great narrative essay make. You also need reflection on the story you are telling—and dialogue and description to bring it to life. You must, as they say, show *and* tell in your college essay.

While other factors such as grades, test scores, and extracurricular activities certainly play an important role in deciding a student's fate, the essay—especially an honest, interesting, beautifully written (though not necessarily perfect) essay—can indeed tip the scales in the student's favor.

I know. I worked in college admissions.

The job of an admissions officer is daunting. To be tasked with the awesome job of deciding who will get in and who will not—now that is a lot of responsibility.

The job of an admissions officer is also (often) boring. She stretches, sighs, takes another sip of coffee, and waits for the inevitable—a big, fat yawn.

I don't mean to be insulting. I mean to make clear that the essays that get students into the colleges of their dreams—or, as I said, at the very least, tip the scales in their favor—must grab the admissions officers by the collar and not let go.

I know that when I read an essay from start to finish, with real interest, compassion, delight, or fascination—if everything else was in order—it was hard to say no.

The essay needs to be gripping (not gimmicky), honest, and unique. The job of the essay is to embody in two dimensions what exists in three—to bring you to life in front of the admissions committee so that they have a real sense of who you are and what you're made of. They want to know how you think, what's important to you, how you handle adversity, where you see yourself headed, and how you deal with the hand you've been dealt, so they can decide whether you would be a good fit for their school. But you can't tell them directly. You must somehow *show* them by writing an essay that embodies your essence.

I can't tell you how many times I've read essays that began, "Last summer I volunteered for organization A, B, or C . . ." and went on to describe in chronological order all the events of the summer, the student touting his or her accomplishments every step of the way.

What makes a great essay great is not a list of accomplishments but a flavor of uniqueness, a glimpse into the life and heart of the writer, an embodiment of a student's *je ne sais quoi.*

And yet, although it is probably the single most important essay a student will ever write in his or her life, the college essay gets sent to admissions offices never to be seen again. Students pour their hearts out in these essays. They spend more time on this particular part of the college application than they do on all the other parts put together. The college essay is the expression and culmination of seventeen years of living on this planet. But when the admissions committee is done reading it, where does it go? What happens to those essays?

We know the answer to that question. They are shredded, tossed into recycling, virtually erased from existence!

The mission of *Best College Essays* is to exhume these diamonds in the rough, destined to be discarded as soon as the process is over, and expose them to the light of day in an effort to mark, showcase, and honor this often overlooked rite of passage.

A byproduct of this worthy goal is that this book provides a plethora of high-quality examples of what a college essay can be or do.

Writing from models is a great way to learn.

I am always amazed at how students respond when I show them sample essays. "You can write about that?" they often say.

They have no idea what a wide (read: infinite) range of topics is available to them. And, as I already mentioned, many have never even seen a narrative essay before.

Best College Essays 2014 offers more than sixty examples—all very different from each other—of essays students have written that got them into the schools of their dreams.

It's not a book to be read from start to finish necessarily—although you are welcome to do so, if you so desire—but to be tapped into, read randomly, even. We did not group the essays in any particular order. We did not put the winning essays or finalists first, though, of course, we have recognized them. Rather, we have organized the essays alphabetically. All of them are equally worthy—although you may prefer one to another.

We have also chosen not to revise the essays in this book. Proofread, yes. Revise, no. What this means is that some of the essays are a little rough around the edges. But remember, we wanted authentic voices telling a real story. We did not want essays written by college counselors, creative writing teachers, and parents. We wanted student voices to be represented as nakedly as possible and to be valued for what they are.

Best College Essays represents submissions from students all over the world applying to American universities. Are these really the *best* essays anywhere out there? They are the best from those we received.

Our judges read hundreds of submissions. As this was the first year of the competition, we are hoping that in the coming year—once this book comes out—the next generation of students will be inspired to write essays they may never have thought possible and submit them to the competition so that they, too (the students and the essays) may stand up and be counted. I am certain that, for every essay we have published, there are tens of thousands of other worthy essays out there. May this book forge the way to stronger, more risk-taking, more open and powerfully written essays to come.

Rather than analyze what worked in each essay, we have let students speak for themselves about the process they went through in writing these essays. Where we could—it was not always possible—we included the prompt and the college that the student plans to attend. Often, when the prompt was not indicated, the essay was a response to Common Application Question #1: *Some students have a background or story that is so central to their identity that they believe their application would be incomplete without it. If this sounds like you, then please share your story.*

You will see in the essays that were chosen moments of brilliance, vulnerability, and self-reflection. You will see heartache and triumph. You will hear voices of students struggling to make sense of the world and to be heard. These essays are artifacts of human consciousness (true for all writing, really). The essays in this anthology, however, give us a glimpse into the dreams, lives, and stories of young adults at the moment they are reaching toward, and about to step into, the world.

The record of these journeys would be lost, like the island of Atlantis, without books such as this one.

I am honored to be part of such an expedition.

Some students have a background or story that is so central to their identity that they believe their application would be incomplete without it. If this sounds like you, then please share your story. (Common Application)

TO LOVE AND BE LOVED

Hannah Ades

The yellow-brimmed tiles bounced the sound off the walls in an incomprehensible, unforgiving way. The cracked windows scattered the light, which always seems so different in Buenos Aires, onto the concrete floors of the public hospital. My mother's face was so astoundingly calm that I almost felt silly every time my throat went dry.

A few months before, I had cried in a dimly lit Sarabeth's on 92nd Street when my mother told me that my maternal grandfather was not related to me. I had always seen myself in Ismael Aizenszlos. I joked that my genes had somehow been passed directly down from him and skipped my mother: our love for dogs, the witty sense of humor we share, and even our penchant for a little extra Parmesan on everything. To feel so closely related to the man I cared about most was a blessing, and I thought myself a better person just for being like him.

My real grandfather, Luis Guimarey, had left my grandmother when my mother was born. Now, as I sat down in the wing of the hospital where he was being treated, I wondered if the man who had once refused to be a part of my mother's life would remind me of myself. I wanted his smile to be like mine and his laugh to remind me of my own. After all, we all want to come from somewhere. On the other hand, I felt foolish, as if I had created an identity for myself by seeing similarities to Ismael that weren't actually there, believing in a figment of my desires.

It was strange to wish to be like someone I had yet to lay eyes on, but in the moments before our meeting, I felt I could not escape being compared to him. He sat down next to me after the reunion with my mother, in which she shed tears I've often wondered about. "Puedo ver tus dibujos?" he said, seemingly undaunted by our first encounter. It dawned on me that my skills as an artist and photographer, which had always gone unaccounted for, might have come from him, from his frail hands and nimble fingers. I wondered how something so simple could have been passed down to me. As my mother learned from infrequent visits to his home and family, he is histrionic, also like me.

I felt as though I were betraying my mother, forgiving his cruelty by wishing for some of his traits to be my own. How could I be like the man who had left my mother with the most sickening memories, shamed and darkened my family history? What did it say about me that I suddenly saw so much of myself in him? I was forced to face what seemed like an unavoidable truth: For better or for worse, he was the one I came from. Did this mean that I was not kindhearted, compassionate, and unvaryingly happy like Ismael? That I was selfish and heartless? I began to see myself in an unflattering light, burdened by all of Luis' unbecoming flaws.

But what if this weren't the way things had to be? I allowed myself to think about the alternatives. "You're who you are because of the way we raised you," said my mom in response to my troubled questions. I then realized that I was taken to the hospital to hear an unspoken truth: My identity was not defined by Luis' reprehensible qualities. Blood relations do not define us or confine us. Rather, we define ourselves by the choices that we make and by the love of those who choose to stay close to us. I now knew where my artistic qualities came from. And yet, I could remain the person who I had been all these years, the person who was raised to love and be loved, to be just like Ismael.

About the Author: I grew up in New York City to Argentinian parents, Spanish being my first language. In college I hope to remain involved in the arts and take an interdisciplinary approach to the study of psychology and theatre. I plan to live my life by seeing the world from every possible perspective and to never allow reality to limit my imagination.

High School Attended: Horace Mann, Bronx, New York

The Process: In order to create this essay, I attempted to understand my identity by exploring the impact of my past experiences and the emotional bond I have to those I love.

Acknowledgments: Mr. Chris Farmer, my school college counselor, for his guidance and support throughout the whole process.

We are interested in learning more about you and the context in which you have grown up, formed your aspirations, and accomplished your academic successes. Please describe the factors and challenges that have most shaped your personal life and aspirations. How have these factors caused you to grow?

THERE IS NOTHING TO FEAR BUT FEAR ITSELF

Sophia Aguirre

"What are you thinking?" he yelled. "They go in the trunk, not the backseat! Listen! Listen when I tell you to do something! Use your head! I don't have time to explain every little thing to you! Think! Go fix it!" And with that, my dad shoved me in the direction of the fishing poles, and I scrambled to get them in the trunk as quickly as possible so he would not yell at me for moving too slowly.

These types of encounters with my dad were a common occurrence. Little misunderstandings would bring out his anger, making my dad the person I feared most. From a young age, I learned to avoid his anger at all costs. Many nights, I would cry myself to sleep and wish more than anything that I could leave his house and never return. But even at that age, I knew that it was not an option.

My parents divorced when I was six. Shortly after, my brother and I began having to split our time between my mom's house and my dad's house. While most kids were celebrating the joy of Fridays, inside, I dreaded every other Friday because I knew that I would have to go to my dad's for the weekend. On those days, I would curl up in my mom's arms, cry, and beg her not to make me go to my dad's again. As much as I wished for a way out, the horn still honked, and I would frantically wipe my tears away and paste on a fake smile as I walked to his car.

Instead of becoming bitter and angry because of my situation, I channeled all my energy into my schoolwork. I used the time spent at my dad's to do homework and to study for the SAT. I would dream about my goal of attending college because I saw my education as my ticket out of my circumstances and as a way to get closer to my goal of becoming a doctor. Getting my degree would not only grant me my independence, but it would also mean that all my years of hard work would finally pay off.

During my freshman year of high school, I finally felt ready to face my fear. I decided to tell my dad how I really felt and that I wanted to spend more time at my mom's house. When I told him, the utter contempt in his eyes was like nothing I had ever seen in anyone before. I instantly became the bad daughter who was ungrateful for everything he had done for me. He combined a dismissiveness of my feelings with disparaging comments about my mother. In that moment, it would have been so easy to cave in to his scathing anger and waiver from my resolve to reduce his visitation time with us. I would have avoided months of struggles by abandoning my true feelings and pretending like everything was fine. I chose not to. In that moment, fear took a backseat and my goal was my driving force.

After many more difficult conversations, my dad finally agreed to participate in counseling sessions with my brother and me, which meant enduring my father's rage and resistance to our wishes. I would be sitting on one couch with tears streaming down my face, and he would be sitting on another screaming at me. It often felt like nothing would ever change. In the end, I earned the biggest reward; his visitation was reduced from fifty percent to thirty percent. Because I am spending less time at my dad's, I no longer feel anxious and stressed all of the time. The time now spent at my dad's house has become more bearable because he knows my true feelings, and I can express myself. It has made all the difference.

Reflecting back on these painful experiences, I find myself feeling the same emotions that I felt as a six-year-old child. My chest still tightens, and tears still threaten to brim over my eyes, but I am no longer the same scared, little girl. By confronting and conquering my biggest fear, I proved to myself that I have control over my own destiny and I will reach my goals. As I look forward to my college experience, although it is somewhat intimidating, I know that it is an opportunity I will fully embrace and take advantage of. It is an opportunity that moves me closer to my goals and one that I have worked hard to earn. This is the ticket I have been waiting for, and nothing, not even fear, is going to stand in my way.

About the Author: My name is Sophia Aguirre, and I live in Tucson, Arizona. My goal is to become an emergency medicine doctor and to attend Stanford University.

High School Attended: Tucson Magnet High School

The Process: I started writing my essay during the summer. I went through about nine drafts before I was satisfied with the outcome, and then I sent it to multiple people and they reviewed it and gave me feedback. I then made changes to my essay with their feedback in mind, and after that I submitted it.

Acknowledgments: Mentor: Karen Ramirez, Mom: Lydia Aguirre

Sophia Aguirre will be attending the University of Arizona

Describe a place or environment where you are perfectly content. What do you do or experience there, and why is it meaningful to you? (Common Application)

THE PHILOSOPHIC MASCOT

Benjamin Aronson

I tentatively step out of the car and feel the breeze coming off of Boston Harbor through my clothes. The mask is already dripping with sweat on the inside, and the thin transparent plastic in front of my eyes fogs up every time I take a heavy, nervous breath. My heart has dropped into my already upside-down stomach, and I haven't even walked into the venue yet. I glance to either side to reassure myself I was still with my friends and to see if they are feeling as nervous as I am. We begin to attract stares and laughs while each group of people we walk by murmurs to their group about how ridiculous we look. I hear one person specifically chuckle, "Those kids have guts." I again look to where my friends should be, but this time I only see a chicken, a bunny, and an M&M wearing a Santa hat. I glance down at myself and remember I am wearing a stormtrooper costume from Star Wars. It hits me, "We are actually doing this." Soon, we are dancing around the throngs of people waiting for the concert to begin, taking pictures with admirers. We stay in one spot while a line of people wait for a photo. Regular, everyday people looking at regular, everyday kids wearing ridiculous costumes. The concert goes by in a montage of flashes and snaps as we dance in outfits that were never meant for dancing. Exhausted, we float back to our car. Completely content, I begin to wonder if there are any other places that could create an equal feeling of happiness and soon, one comes to me.

The air around me is musty and stale for it hasn't seen air flow in years. The only visible light comes from a small fish tank in the back of the room. Filled with pizza and soda from our recent trip to our favorite restaurant, my same friends sitting near me blend into the impervious darkness and complete the feeling of being lost in space. Words flow directly out of our minds rather than complicate themselves in the worries of everyday life. It is dubbed, "The Philosophy Room." The smallest insecurities in our high school lives to the intricate thoughts of the greatest philosophical principles are debated in the basement of a friend's house. Thoughts can be spoken without any judgments as we disconnect ourselves from stressful worries and free our minds, a sort of meditation occurs. Eventually, a time comes when we must leave this perfect place, and we must return to our daily life.

In both environments, the idea of living in the present is more prevalent than at any other point in my life. As humans speed through life constantly focusing on the next event on their schedule, I have attempted to delay the inevitability of years passing uncontrollably by. The world I live in is based on the high-speed necessity of millions of things, yet wearing a ridiculous costume for a few hours or philosophizing about life brings to me a profound awareness. Being able to do so with a clear mind, free of any intoxicating substances, allows me to induce the purest and deepest emotions possibly created. While many share their wildest stories whilst intoxicated beyond repair, I strive to achieve the same success as a completely clean and sober person. In my eyes, happiness is not permanent, and these environments mean more than just an escape from the business of the real world. They allow me to feel as if happiness is never ending, even for just a few hours. More importantly, they let me be the most successful person there can be in the world, someone who is happy.

About the Author: My name is Ben Aronson, I live in Longmeadow, Massachusetts, with my mother, father, and younger sister. My goal in life is to inspire and help others in some way.

High School Attended: Longmeadow, MA

The Process: The topics discussed in the essay are ones that I rarely talk about in person, so I felt as if putting them on paper could really help describe them to myself or others. Instead of fretting about my writing style or word choice, I let the thoughts flow onto the page.

Ben Aronson will be attending University of Maryland, College Park.

HOTEL GYPSY

Josie Baker—Finalist

I was an adolescent hotel gypsy. Perhaps hotel nomad would be a more accurate term seeing as my family and I had been moving from hotel to motel and back again for two years.

Our "clan" consisted of my father, my younger sister Deirdre, my (half) brother Warren, and I. When we began staying in hotels, it seemed like a vacation: fun and ephemeral. We merely had to entertain ourselves when my dad did not want us around. We swam, and when Warren got bored, we played Spy in the deserted hallways. It was certainly different from life at home with our mother. Cramped into one hotel room, we could not get away from each other. While at my mom's I could go a week without seeing her, and it felt like I had no family, but at hotels I could not escape my family.

As my dad went downhill, so did the hotels. We stayed everywhere from Marriott to Motel Six. Once we stayed in a hotel where a window was blown out. All through the night, frigid air blew through our room, and we clutched our blankets like they were our last salvation. After this nomadic era, my dad left for Seattle and cut off contact with us completely. I thought my time as a hotel gypsy was over. Last winter, however, while I was home from seeking my own adventures in Philadelphia, my dad returned, expecting Deirdre and me to drop everything and spend Christmas in a hotel with him. Out of love, we did.

It was five o'clock Christmas morning. I woke, not out of excitement, but from the anxiety that constantly plagued me when staying with my dad. I gazed across the hotel room; there he lay, in a booze-enhanced slumber, snoring like a rhinoceros. "Go back to sleep!" my brain screamed, but looking at my sister adjacent to me, I could not. Despite the abhorrent hour in the morning, I rose from my bed, sidestepped piles of clothing and paper plates from the night before and went looking for gifts. I found, and sorted the presents—for Deirdre, a delicate gold necklace, and for me, a hip purse. I thanked some higher power that at least he had bought wrapping paper. After hours of toiling over gifts, I had a pile of meticulously wrapped presents and stockings filled to the brim with chocolate. I even included my father's signature touch of labelling the biggest presents "From: Santa." Now all I needed was a Christmas tree. Scanning the room, I settled on an art deco lamp, on which I could hang the stockings. I lay the presents below and hung the stockings with care, hoping my sister would believe our father had been there. Afterwards, I travelled downstairs to the gift shop to add my own personal touch by buying Deirdre's favorite candy: Reese's Peanut Butter Cups. Eventually my father and sister, late risers, awoke and Christmas commenced. Seeing my sister so happy, I knew I had done something special. I felt like one of Santa's elves.

When my dad made eye contact with me and mouthed the words, "Thank you," as Deirdre unwrapped her final present, I averted my gaze. My cheeks flushed as I realized how embarrassed I was for him. I was substitute dad again; it was disquieting.

I have not talked to my dad since, but not for lack of trying. I do not discuss our time as "hotel gypsies" except with my sister, and when I do, what we recall is our collection of hotel key cards, continental breakfasts, and swimming pools drained for maintenance. It was not a happy two years for my family, or a sad two years, more like an extraordinarily long roller coaster where ultimately you felt sick. I feel stronger now, not like a nomad, but like a traveler.

About the Author: My name is Josie. I am from Oakland, California. I have had a complicated family past but it does not define me, it only makes me stronger.

High School Attended: Orinda Academy, Orinda, CA

The Process: I sat down one day and just sort of blurted out my experiences onto the computer. Then after multiple rounds of my college counselor editing my essay and having my English teacher look it over, I had this gem of an essay.

Acknowledgments: Gabrielle Glancy

Josie Baker will be attending Reed College. She got in Early Decision.

WHY REED?

Josie Baker—Finalist

I grew up in a community of intelligent, ambitious, and unconventional thinkers: Reedies. They taught me that all culture has value and that all knowledge is worthwhile. My parents, who were Reedies, and their friends, were some of my favorite people because they could do everything from juggle five balls at once to explain exponents. To my younger self, these were the most amazing skills in the world. As time went by I continued to be in awe of the adults in my life. They taught me the law of thirds in photography and the complicated reasons behind the national concern over the H1N5 virus jump. Reedies joke about their motto being "Communism, Atheism and Free Love." So, my mom's live-in boyfriend, Joe, may be a communist, neither of my parents believe in God, and my mom and Joe plan on being together forever without getting married, BUT, I do not think that is what Reed is about. Reed is about the intellectual spirit. Reed is about learning for its own sake, not for grades or class standing.

I was lucky enough to be raised by (a lot of) Reedies, but that is not the main reason I wish to become one. I was never pressured by my parents to go to Reed. In fact, they were entirely indifferent. I looked at other schools, lots of other schools, hoping not to seem like I was conforming by following in my parents' footsteps. With every college visit there was still a voice in the back of my head saying "Well, it's nice, but Reed is better." I can't help it. When I toured Reed, the tour guide was candid while being upbeat and positive. She shared anecdotes of late nights at the library and Renn Fayre. She was not fake or too perky, just honest and amiable, and she did not utter the fateful words that I have heard from too many female tour guides: "Math just isn't my thing."

I abhor the phrase "math just isn't my thing" because math just is my thing. I am unapologetically a math geek. I relish the opportunity to help calculus students with their homework and am in awe that by using calculus one can find the area between two equations and then find the volume those equations would create if rotated about the x or y axis.

I now care about school, which may not be socially acceptable or the average teen's definition of "cool," but I do. I love it when I stay up until one a.m. writing three essays and only two of them are in English. I feel adept and intelligent. I enjoy academics because I have a thirst for knowledge. I am insatiably curious. That is why I belong at Reed.

About the Author: My name is Josie and I am from Oakland, California.

High School Attended: Orinda Academy, Orinda, CA

The Process: This essay was one of those "struck by inspiration" pieces. I wrote it all in one sitting, and with limited edits and a little bit of help from my college counselor, it was perfected.

Josie Baker will be attending Reed College. She got in Early Decision.

WALKING WITHOUT CEREAL

Mason Bartle – Finalist

"Hey, if you guys don't give me your cereal, I'm going to beat you up!"

That was what I heard when I was walking to the local pastry shop with my friend two summers ago. As we rounded the first corner, a ragged-looking man in his late thirties with a strange look in his eye came up to us and attempted to mug us for a box of Cheerios that neither of us was holding. We looked at the man blankly, and after a couple of seconds, both muttered a confused "What?" He looked at us menacingly and said, "Nah, that ain't funny." For a split second, my friend and I stood still, utterly confused, until the man broke into a wide grin, looked off in the distance, and said, "Yeah it is!" before completely ignoring us and walking away.

Though I'll admit I was a little unnerved by the encounter, I never came close to being outright frightened. That's because my city has taught me to expect the unexpected and to react to unusual situations. Utica, New York is a strange place. As cheesy as it may sound, my nearly eighteen years in this city have truly shaped me to become the person I am today. The lessons Utica has taught me have made me very happy here, and when I walk around the streets, I feel a sense of comfort and belonging.

It's amazing how assimilated the different cultures of Utica are. It's because of this proximity to these cultures that I, a middle-class, embarrassingly white boy, started listening to, enjoying, and even relating to rap and hip-hop. And perhaps most importantly, it's because of this proximity that an atheist like me began to understand and appreciate the importance of all the world's religions for lending people a sense of comfort and shared culture. I shudder to think of the condescending, arrogant man I might have become if I had grown up in an area where that kind of understanding was harder to come by.

I like to walk around Utica. I've explored the nooks and crannies of this city and its environs since I learned to walk. My excursions into its marshes, parks, cemeteries, and public buildings have developed my sense of curiosity and have led to a series of intriguing conversations with my friends, as we debate whether pieces of asphalt in one of the marshes suggest the existence of an abandoned and long-forgotten road, or why there are steps in the park that lead to nowhere. Occasionally, our conversations digress from our surroundings and we begin to talk about our mutual love for the sciences. One of my friends loves to talk about biology and anatomy. Another talks to me about philosophy and theoretical physics. Yet another discusses chemistry with me, and we often begin to plan some sort of grand chemical experiment, like making an artificial flavor from scratch. Due to the inevitable flammability of some important ingredients, however, our plans often fall flat.

Though I love Utica, and enjoy nearly every minute I spend here, the sense of curiosity and exploration that it has given me has also given me the desire to leave and explore the world around me. I plan to bring this spirit of inquiry, exploration, and discussion to college with me. Wherever I go, I'll be the first to start up conversations about the Higgs boson or tetrachromacy in humans. I know that I will learn as much or more from my surroundings in college as I have in Utica, and the prospect excites me. I can't wait to experience the next crazy situation the world throws at me.

And I'll be sure to carry around some cereal, just in case.

About the Author: Though I was officially born in the small town of Hamilton, New York, I have lived all my life in the nearby city of Utica. My experiences here have led to my interest in physics, biology, and music. I hope to enter a career in the sciences after college.

High School Attended: T. R. Proctor High School, Utica, New York

The Process: I stared at a screen trying to think of something grand to write. I thought for hours before I realized that the best way to tackle the essay was to simply tell a story.

Acknowledgments: John Bartle; Alison, Edward, and Andrea Doughtie; Danielle Brain; Rebecca Nix; and Stacy Dawes for reviewing my essay.

Mason Bartle will be attending Brown University.

A Dark Place Is
My Happy Place

Natalya Brill

No distractions or pressure, just the darkness wrapped around me and my photo negative. I am content in a darkroom.

When I first signed up in 2010 to take a color film photography course, I had no idea how to use a film camera and had never spent more than a few minutes in a pitch-black room. Working uninterrupted for hours in a chilly, lightless room terrified and excited me.

Since then, the darkroom has become my sanctuary, a place where I am not sidetracked by responsibilities from the outside world. Not bothered by my AP English essay or need to drive the soccer ball up the field during a game or my duty as the Peer Leader Club president to come up with the concept for our next fundraiser. Whether I take one or fifty times to get the photo print right, nothing in the moment can divert my concentration.

I have spent hundreds of Saturday mornings and afternoons tracking down subjects and hovering over enlargers, deciding which film negative to print next. The process of shooting, developing, and printing photographs is invigorating. I have found a new way of looking at ordinary moments and communicating those revelations to my family, friends, and others in my life.

Before I take a photograph, I construct a visual image in my mind. Mood is what I'm after—I try using different objects and angles to see what flows and connects together, just as I experiment with a variety of words and phrases in advance of putting a verse to paper. My point of view doesn't usually become clear to me until the photograph is finished.

The majority of the magic, however, takes place within the darkroom. In the beginning, I would always shiver as I stepped foot into the room, and the chilly air wrapped itself around me. Using only my hands to see, I felt incredibly inferior to the darkness. Now, I relish the isolation and silence in anticipation of watching my photo finish soaking in the tub of chemicals.

I feel a greater satisfaction taking and developing photos in black and white than color. I want my artwork to receive the viewer's full attention to details and composition. A colorless photograph's aesthetic appeal lies in its intensity; color can be distracting. With black and white, nuances matter more. To get that right, darkroom technique is imperative.

Given the instant feedback I'm so used to in this hyper world, I am grateful for the patience that photography demands before my final product emerges. The images I capture rarely are exactly what I expect they would be, and usually the ones I am most proud of expand upon my original intentions in surprising ways.

There are countless ways to enthrall a person and present a message. During the week, I mainly communicate with words. These may be delivered quickly or leisurely, but the point to be made is usually handed to the recipient. With photography, the viewer's perception can change the meaning of the image. I may not ever know what he or she takes away from my work, but as long as I can prod someone to think, I welcome the mystery.

Behind the walls of the darkroom, the isolation and unique focus bring me absolute contentment. As I emerge into the light, once again, my attention shifts to the demands of my busy world.

About the Author: Living in New York City for seventeen years, I have never had an excuse to be bored as there are countless things to do. One goal in my life is just to experience living in a city totally and utterly different than NYC.

High School Attended: NYC, NY

The Process: I spent about three brutal, never-ending months on this essay. At first, I wasn't really comfortable writing about myself. Typically, in my English courses, I was taught to write in a flowery manner rather than straightforward and to the point, so it was a strange transition. I learned more and more about myself as I sat down every day picking into the depths of my brain in hopes of discovering "what place/environment makes me content." All in all, I believe the work I put in was worth the outcome and the ends justified the means.

Acknowledgments: My Family

Natalya Brill will be attending Union College.

Some students have a background or a story that is so central to their identity that they believe their application would be incomplete without it. If this sounds like you, then please share your story.

NOMAD

Andrea Canizares-Fernandez

I turn over in bed; lemon rays hit my eyelids through the window, and in one soft breath, the smell of mowed grass splits my foggy morning thoughts in half. I scrunch my eyelashes, stretch my toes, and lie there in expectation, clinging to this scent for as long as I can. All of a sudden I'm in Buffalo. My world is one street: Stevenson Boulevard. In front live the twins, who've taught me everything about baseball, hockey, and friendship. To my left live little Stephanie and the rest of her sugarplum sweet, Christian family. On the right is the old lady with the garden full of valentine flowers that always droop into our backyard. I grip to this faded smell because with a kaleidoscope view, I recall the first of many houses that felt like home. My room, where I'd dance around in my princess pajamas and catch autumn leaves from my window, chasing my brother down the stairs during a game of Pokémon or coming down for enchilada dinner. Often I close my eyes and hear my father telling us stories in Spanish, my mom humming in the kitchen, and my brother and I sitting attentively by his feet.

The recollection recedes as I think of Boston. With my face in the pillow, I picture our cramped apartment with cold cement floors and a room that barely fit our sibling bunk bed, making us physically and emotionally closer. How my mother, due to her job, was gone most of the time. I almost hear the ring of my father's mountain bike with that yellow, child carrier behind, pulling my brother to karate and me to ballet every single afternoon. I stifle a yawn and recall Los Angeles, the hefty, beige house full of windows. I plainly see the smile of my best friend Sabrina, the nights we spent playing with my hamster and reading Junie B. Jones. It was the place that introduced me to school cliques and warmer winters.

I have lived in 8 states and 13 houses. For years this statement was my refrain, and I would hardly think about the weight of my words as I spoke. But recently I have been dipping nostalgically into my past and have realized the significance of this sentence. Both my parents are originally from Ecuador. For political reasons, in 1987, they were forced to uproot their lives and build themselves a home in the United States. Slowly my father climbed the professional ladder, eventually becoming a history professor and a reputable author. Although this was a great success story for my father, the rest of our family was forced to follow him across the country as he rose in importance. We traveled from Wisconsin to New Jersey to Rhode Island to Texas, picking up our lives and moving into a new funny-smelling, yearly rental before we could even try to settle in.

Every place I've lived is not just a hazy morning thought; it is a blueprint to who I am. As a child, I didn't understand how much our nomadic tendencies altered my life. But now in retrospect, I see a flip-book of endless goodbyes. This idea of my past might sound bitter—and on some level it is. I've never liked change, but I can also acknowledge how every home has molded me. Each place has been a new and different adventure, and I can't imagine my identity without each story. Throughout my life, I have been exposed to a myriad of faces, cultures, and anecdotes. I've been forced into quick adaptation and through that I know how to open up to others and make friends quickly. I have learned to hold onto what I love, and hold on tightly. I've lived in 8 states and 13 houses, and I know now that every single home takes a different and valuable part of my heart.

About the Author: My name is Andrea Canizares-Fernandez, and I live in Austin, Texas. I aspire to someday become an actress, singer, and environmentalist.

High School Attended: Liberal Arts and Science Academy (Lasa) High School, Austin, TX

The Process: When I read the prompt, I immediately knew what I wanted to write about. I know that my constant moving as a child is central to my identity, and so I felt that I needed to somehow include that aspect of my life in my application. The words came easily, and with the help of a few trusted adults, I added necessary imagery and polished the piece.

Acknowledgments: My dad, my college counselor, Ms. Kocian, and my English teachers—Mr. Harry and Mr. Snyder.

Describe a place or environment where you are perfectly content. What do you do or experience there and why is it meaningful to you? (Common Application)

MY HAPPY PLACE

Ashley Castillo – Finalist

I sit in a small room surrounded by dust, screws and more tools than I can name, staring at the numbers on my computer screen. I hear hammers hitting nails, saws cutting wood, and men talking in loud, deep voices. I listen as one of the guys accepts a package from Home Depot as I enter the latest receipts for the department of buildings permits. Here, is where every part of the company comes together.

Last summer, I started working as a bookkeeper for Manhattanville Restoration LLC., a construction company. We currently have three houses in construction—for each construction site, I maintain weekly ledgers and create status reports of labor hours and activities. I record a total of about $1.2 million in transactions into an Excel spreadsheet. At the end of each week, I meet with the CEO to go over how much money was spent, what was done, and whether or not we need to be wired more money from the investor. It's a ton of responsibility, but the responsibility and leadership involved in my job is what I'm most passionate about.

People often ask why I want to spend the rest of my life looking at numbers and doing math. They make it sound boring, but I don't see it that way. Sure, math has always been my favorite subject, and it's something I enjoy; however, finances are only one part of a business. That's what I love about my job. I'm firstly responsible for recording transactions and filing receipts, but it's not all I do. I act as the eyes of the working men as they carry large pieces of sheet rock over their heads, sign for delivery packages, guide inspectors as they survey the property, and even have lunch with the CEO and investor of the company.

The financial part of my job isn't just entering numbers into a spreadsheet, either. Every tired man represents the labor and human capital of a project, every receipt the raw materials and inputs for a product, and every finished and sold home the result of all the months of hard work. This is amazing to me. I get an opportunity to observe a business and its projects from start to finish. I also get to see this small business thrive in a time when such few new companies survive. And I can learn from what they do right as well as what they do wrong. Business owners are often so preoccupied with the more technical parts of their companies, like finances and regulations, that they don't get to see the smaller parts that make up the product—but are crucial to the company's process. I, however, get to observe these parts every day and use my observations to help this company—and my own one day— succeed.

As I sit and enter receipts, I get distracted by the headline on the newspaper my boss had been reading that morning. It says "Housing Market Is Heating Up, if Not Yet Bubbling." I know that when people say a market is "bubbling," it doesn't usually end well; it means prices are rising so high that they are above the product's actual value. The prices rise until the "bubble" bursts, causing a dramatic drop in prices and negative effects on the economy. But this headline is still reassuring to me— I find it refreshing that economists are predicting such a fate for the housing market while I'm helping Manhattanville Restoration LLC. thrive. It shows me that businesses can succeed, even when chances seem slim, thanks to proper management and decision-making. As if reading my mind, my boss comes in as I finish the article and tells me the good news: the house that we finished constructing only four weeks ago was sold.

About the Author: Ashley Castillo lives in Bronx, NY. She is treasurer of her school's Student Government and National Honor Society chapter. In the distant future, she looks forward to studying business and becoming a CEO.

High School Attended: NEST+m High School New York, NY

The Process: When writing this essay, I thought of what experiences made me stand out from other applicants. This is something that takes up so much of my time and I have become so passionate about. It is also something that has prepared me for my future career. While writing the essay, I kept these things in mind and just let my interest and personality shine through as I told my story.

Acknowledgments: Special thank you to Ashley Mateo, Blaise Goswami, as well as the rest of the Minds Matter team for their help and guidance while writing this essay.

Ashley Castillo will be attending The Wharton School of Business, University of Pennsylvania.

A LITTLE LESS LAZY

Gerardo Castillo

Walking on dirt and gravel, feet sore, and fatigued from the strenuous journey, my mother finally caught a glimpse of what would be her future in the United States. I come from a family of immigrants who risked their lives to come to America as a way of salvation from the indigent conditions they had back home. My mother resorted to the only way to attain a more desirable life by moving to the US because conditions in her hometown of Plenitud, Zacatecas, were not suitable. She struggled to adapt to a whole different environment in the United States. It is one that is unforgiving to immigrants, yet she managed to pull through by juggling her jobs while raising a child and learning a foreign language. I admire my mother for her perseverance and strength, traits that I have gained after enduring a rough childhood.

I grew up in a different neighborhood compared to others. I lived in a trailer home with my mother, grandmother, and sister since it was the only thing that we could afford. It can be difficult at times being Latino because of our ideals, which emphasize hard work but never place much focus on obtaining a higher education. Most of my old friends that live in my neighborhood engraved that motto into their heads and stuck with it. Instead of focusing on school, they placed more attention towards getting out of school; some resorted to drugs and alcohol just to fit in. I had to cut my ties with them since I did not want to fall under the same stupor. Through their mistakes, it dawned on me that I did not want to end up like they did, hopeless and without a certain future. I let go of my old friends, but I managed to find better ones that have the same common goals and interests as me. I met these new friends when I started to attend the Preuss School UCSD, a school that focuses on helping low-income students have a chance to attend college.

About the Author: I live in San Diego and my goal in life is to repay my mother by making something out of my life.

Acknowledgments: My teacher and best friend/mentor

HOW MATH CAN HELP SHAPE THE WORLD

Aviva Chaidell — Finalist

Drive 14 miles on the Saw Mill Parkway to the Cross County Parkway, take 4 side roads, and go through 8 traffic lights. Exit on the right side, merge onto North Avenue, and my brother's school is on the left. When I was 3, my dad took me on this route every day and after just a few times, I knew it by heart. I couldn't read street signs, but that didn't stop me from giving directions. I remembered the way to go by seeing the streets in relation to each other. I see the world through a math lens, and my strong visual-spatial skills have always allowed me to give solid directions.

I am dyslexic, so my brain doesn't function like a "normal" brain. I have a math brain. I take the 7 bus to the 1 train, switch to the 2 or 3 train, then take the 7 train to the 6 train and walk 1 street and 3 avenues to get to my high school in midtown Manhattan. Since Manhattan is a grid, my math and directional skills are helpful and allow me to make my way around the city easily. Once I go somewhere new, I have a blueprint of the route, so I always reference it to figure out where I am going. It's like I have my own built-in GPS and can give directions with the accuracy of the iPhone maps app.

When I was in high school, I realized that the world around me was language oriented. At the Everett Children's Adventure Garden in The New York Botanical Garden, there was a certain way of explaining each station at which I worked. My supervisor gave me a script, but I changed some words to add more steps so I could use math. For example, when I showed children how to pot a plant, I would give them step-by-step directions, like telling them to squirt the plant 15 times with water.

In school, having to read textbooks, novels, and take standardized tests has made my life challenging. My brain has to look at words in a different way to try to understand them in a number form. At first, some might think that having a math brain might be negative, but it has helped me see things in a different way.

In the math classroom, I feel perfect in every way. On the 4th floor in room 404, I learn math skills that I carry with me today. Time goes quickly in math class because it is a place where I can be comfortable and stress-free. Some people think math is boring or pointless because you don't use the quadratic formula every day. I, however, use the skills and knowledge from math class and apply them to everyday life.

I use my number sense to help me with other subjects like history and English. When studying geography, I learn the location of 1 main country and then figure out where other surrounding countries are in relation to it. For example, 2 countries west of India is Iran, 1 country north of that is Nepal, and 3 countries east of India is Thailand. In English class, when I have trouble reading a book, I calculate the number of pages that I have left until the chapter is over. Since I know how many pages I have to read, it gives me more motivation to finish it.

I don't just use math in school, but also in the real world. Even though I am growing up, I will always be that little 3-year-old giving my parents directions. Knowing the way to my brother's school made me realize that I have skills that other people might not have. I can see the world through a math lens and being good at math allows me to be who I am.

About the Author: My name is Aviva Chaidell and I live in Riverdale, NY. My goal in life is to work for a company to do their statistics.

High School Attended: The Churchill School and Center, New York, New York

The Process: First, I talked to my college counselor about what is special about me. She said you love math, and I didn't realize that it was a big part of me. I wrote a rough draft and I got a lot of people to edit and help me make it the best essay.

Acknowledgments: : Erin Hugger, college counselor; Sue Dodell, Mom; Katherine Adams, English teacher; Amber Bergeron, English teacher.

Aviva Chaidell will be attending American University.

BEYOND THE CURLS

Aditi Cherian

"Your hair used to be so straight and nice. What happened? What on earth did you do to it?"

Comments such as these, made by classmates and friends alike, broke my confidence. Like many girls my age, I didn't like the way I looked—mostly, in my case, because of my hair. I thought if I could get my hair to be straight, I would at least look decent. In my mind, straight hair was neat and professional. The kind of hair I had—wild and unruly—made me feel like a jungle animal. Or at least that's what I thought other people were thinking when they looked at me.

Embarrassed, ashamed even, of that mess on top of my head, I decided to try to tame the beast. The hairdresser tugged and tugged. Pulling this way and that. When she was done, I was thoroughly humiliated. All I wanted to do was run and hide. There I was sitting with hair as big as a bird's nest while there were four other women in chairs alongside me who looked great. Straight, wavy, or perfectly textured ringlets—it didn't matter. They didn't have what I had for hair. I stared at myself in the large mirror in front of me and began to cry.

I started straightening my hair in the eighth grade, and I never left the house without making sure every hair was in place. Eventually I realized that the hours I spent straightening my hair was time I could have spent studying or being with my family. Before I came to my senses and accepted myself, I took every look, every glance, and every stare as a criticism. It was hard to let go of all of the insecurities I had about my hair, and it took a certain kind of determination to do so. I had to constantly tell myself that I was not going to use black hair ties, black bobby pins, or a straightener. Each of those items tamed, constrained, and hid the real me, and I was not going to allow that anymore. It wasn't easy; my hands itched from wanting to hide my hair, but, slowly, day by day, I starting to gain strength. I stopped caring so much about what people thought, stopped going against the grain of who I was, and started going with it.

The pivotal point was a visit with my grandparents in Kerala, India. Where they live is lush and green. Banana trees, coconut trees, jack fruit and jasmine. One day while we were there, I looked out the window downstairs and saw my grandmother drying her hair. Her head was bent, and her long, thick, black hair went all the way down to her waist. What I noticed most was the texture. Her hair was a beautiful cascade of endless curls. At that moment I knew where my hair came from, I knew what my hair stood for, and I knew a little more about who I was. My hair came from my grandmother on my dad's side. It represents my heritage. Now I see that I am a unique girl with roots in the beautiful land of Kerala.

I now walk with my head held high and with a slight spring in my step. Letting go of the hang-ups I had about my hair, I unleashed a kind of fearlessness within myself. If I was able to get over years of insecurity over my hair, I could definitely do anything I put my mind to. I began to possess a kind of confidence in myself that I did not have before, and with it came a new catch phrase: I can.

About the Author: I live in Fremont, CA, and go to Mission San Jose High School. My goals in life include becoming a pediatrician, and hopefully starting a business.

High School Attended: Mission San Jose High School ,Fremont, CA

The Process: I first did a free write where I wrote down all my thoughts, and then I started to take the best pieces out and edit to make it perfect.

Some students have a background or story that is so central to their identity that they believe their application would be incomplete without it. If this sounds like you, then please share your story.

TROPICAL BREEZE TO THE BUSY STREETS

Aria Collins

The beautiful sunny beaches and everlasting green grass is where I grew up. It was a place I called home, a place where some people would consider "behind God's back." This place has few opportunities but is plentiful in luscious fruits and vegetables. It is known for its spices, culture, and beauty. At only 344 square kilometers, this is my home. This is the Caribbean, my home is Grenada. Growing up surrounded by beauty and in an environment where even our cooking is an art, it was in my destiny to be an artistic and creative individual.

There is an inherent part of me that enjoys dancing, writing stories, acting, and singing. Growing up, I took part in several activities; it all started when I begged my mother to enroll me in piano lessons and to let me sing at my school and church choir. Aside from my musical passions, I enjoyed ribbon and modern dancing. However, out of all my creative aspects, one of my most memorable moments was performing a skit I wrote in the second grade, entitled "Who is Sasha?" It was about a girl who was a bully and did poorly in school, but in the end everyone spoke to her and influenced her to become a better person.

Enjoying life is amazing, but when living "behind God's back," I realized that none of my passions could have been a reality. My small, sweet, beautiful home was not the land of opportunities. In Grenada you have to compete for basic standard jobs such as a businessman or office clerk. If you studied hard and had the money you would have a better chance of being a doctor or lawyer. These types of jobs did not interest me. I knew I wanted a job where I can be creative and express my ideas and feelings while having fun.

As a child growing up in Grenada, attending a specific college based on your interests and having a future was the last thing on your mind. Sadly, in Grenada, there are several students my age who still have not thought about attending college because they depend on the basic routines and roles that Grenada has. However, I knew I could not fall into routine. My creativity and spontaneity define me.

Leaving my hometown was difficult for me, it was like leaving paradise. On the last day I cried all night. Living for the moment was exciting, no teenager in Grenada cared about their interests and how it can play an important role in your future. We just planned to fit into society and have a simple job. My first move was to St. Thomas for a few months. Not knowing what to experience next was nerve wrecking, but I made it through.

After living in St. Thomas for a few months, I find myself in the land of opportunities, also known as the concrete jungle; a place where people say your dreams can come true. My family lived in a 1.5 bedroom apartment with five household members. A scarcity of food and lack of space has not stopped my love for this city. As time progressed, I rediscovered that writing, film, dancing, acting, and singing will always be my passions; I can make it into my future career.

Today, I consider myself to be an ambitious, dedicated, and a determined young lady. Out of all my interests, I love script writing and film producing the most. Had I not moved to New York, I would have never discovered all of my passions can be found in writing and film producing. New York made me discover that film producing has a little touch of everything I love. I have learned that I can adjust to any environment and be able to follow my dreams and passions until I reach my destiny.

About the Author: I live in Brooklyn, New York. I am a city girl who grew up in the Caribbean. My goals are to become a successful individual. I would like to see my name shining somewhere one day. I would like to be a film producer or work in any department in the field of media. My goal is to be happy with whatever I do and become financially stable in life. I would also like to make my family, friends, and hometown proud every step of the way.

High School Attended: George Westinghouse High School, Brooklyn, NY

The Process: I did it over my last summer in my Pace-Upward Bound Program. Every single day, for at least one hour a day, I sat at the computer and wrote. I started off by free writing, and as time progressed I found my story. It finally began to look like an essay. However, I went through several drafts before it was completed. I had more than three people review my drafts, and I took everyone's opinion into consideration until I made my final successful draft. It took me hard work and determination, but I did my best and wrote one of my most beautiful essays ever.

Acknowledgments: Mr. Sean Callaway, Ms. Sydney Cresap, and Ms. Karina Avila.

Aria Collins will be attending Ithaca College.

LONELINESS AND BEING ALONE

Kayla Cottingham

I'm often struck by how people react to the notion of being solitary—the way a friend's mother's lip curls when you say you're an only child, the uncomfortable shuffle of an acquaintance's feet when you recount a story about your only grade school friend, the raise of eyebrows when you note that you enjoyed the class of only one teacher in freshman year. The same string of thought weaves through the minds of each of these people—more often than not, being the only in a world of many doesn't bode well in the eyes of others. When I describe being alone, they see only loneliness.

Of course, I had a similar belief until one frigid morning in August when I was attending school as an exchange student in New Zealand. The school featured a campus that extended one kilometer from the common rooms to the gymnasium, with subject-specific buildings scattered across the hilly green landscape. Walking from one class to the next could take ten minutes, a far cry from my tiny private school in the States where the farthest walk between classes was down a flight of stairs and twelve steps in either direction. In the States, the halls were crowded and packed tightly with kids pushing others out of the way to get to their next class—in New Zealand, I could look across the field towards the building I was aiming for and only spot five other students heading towards the same place.

That particular morning, those five other students walked in a clump with their heads bent towards a central point while their leather shoes beat down the frozen grass in sync as if they were one collective machine.

Where I stood atop the hill looking down at them, I could see the smiles on their faces, the way their eyebrows sloped and spiked with each passing comment, and the passive brushing of their hands on each other's sleeves, as if they were the intermingling teeth of cogs. From fifteen meters away, I could hear their laughter penetrating the dull violin song humming from my iPod.

For a long minute, I stood in place looking out at the tracks the five of them left in the glittering frost, and I wondered why I wasn't part of a group like theirs. There were a million answers to my rhetorical question—I was an American, I'd only been at their school for three weeks, I had a tendency to befriend a fraction of my classmates instead of a whole—but what did it matter? I asked myself that question, and the nearly comical existential moment hit me:

I was perfectly content to walk from drama to agriculture by myself. I was okay with not growing up in a house full of siblings. I thought grade school was perfect with one friend, because that one friend meant everything to me. I looked back fondly at the one class—and teacher—I liked in freshman year, because amidst a sea of clamoring students and lessons, I walked into that classroom every day excited to be taught by someone who treated me like an individual, not a test average.

That was the difference between being alone and being lonely. I'd spent my entire life being alone in one sense or another—alone at home when my parents left for work, alone in class without my one friend, alone in high school as the only student who foolishly only cared about one subject—and I'd been perfectly happy with it. I liked the silence between the commotions. I liked snuggling up with a book full of vivacious characters in an otherwise empty house, I liked waiting for my best friend on the playground, and I liked being the first one to arrive in English class with a smile on my face. I may have been alone, but I wasn't lonely.

About the Author: My name is Kayla Cottingham. I'm eighteen years old. I live in Salt Lake City, Utah, and my greatest goal in life is to become a best-selling novelist.

High School Attended: Rowland Hall School, Salt Lake City, Utah, USA

The Process: I had multiple brainstorms with English teachers and my college counselor about possible subjects for an essay that really summed me up as a person and, with their help, I came up with the idea of writing about my introversion and explaining why it shouldn't be considered stigmatized. I was answering the question: Describe a place or environment where you are perfectly content. What do you do or experience there, and why is it meaningful to you?

Acknowledgments: I'd like to thank my college counselor, Bruce Hunter, and my junior and senior English teachers, Kody Partridge and Carolyn Hickman, for helping me through the process of writing this essay.

My Grandfather's Stories

Irina Duican

"Ceausescu si poporul! Ceausescu P-C-R!" The heavy chants of the booming crowd reverberated off the small TV in the middle of the dark room. My mother and her parents sat in the cold, watching the dictator of the Romanian Communist regime, Nicolae Ceausescu, speak in front of an acquiescent crowd gathered in the capital's biggest plaza.

A strange, wistful sadness took over my grandfather's expression, as he painfully recounted that scene to me. I visit my family in Romania every summer, and it was a tradition for me and my grandpa to dig out dusty decades-old photographs of my mom and aunt. They always prompted my grandfather to recall memories from the darkest time in his life and tell me stories of the mental suffering and humiliation that he and his family had to endure during the harsh Communist regime.

As we sat at the round kitchen table drinking chamomile tea, my grandpa told me how his daughters attended public schools that taught Communist propaganda and a falsified Romanian history, how no freedom of expression was allowed, and how children were shaped into conforming, identical citizens. To give their kids exposure to real education, he described the long searches he and my grandma did in small bookstores to find rare, great literature to fill their bookshelves. Even though it was a hot, stuffy summer night, my grandpa shivered as he remembered the freezing theaters to which he took his daughters to see Shakespeare and Ibsen plays.

Conditions under the Communist regime were harshly egalitarian, as everyone outside the political elite was given the same allotments of food and money. My grandmother's routine was to wait in cold, crowded supermarket lines to purchase the family's meager food rations. As my grandpa spoke about their struggles to supply basic necessities for the family, I could see the toll that the years of unceasing dedication and hard work had taken on him.

My grandfather stared blankly ahead as he remembered one particular decision he had to make. The Communist Party was always looking for new recruits, and many people joined because of the economic security that was promised. My grandpa knew that refusing this offer would mean no possibility of professional advancement for him and inevitable financial hardship for his family, but his core beliefs never allowed him to become a member of the party.

As my grandfather was finishing his story, I realized how my family's past, and the people they have become because of it, has influenced my upbringing and the values and traits I have come to embody. My belief in the importance of a solid education, my work ethic, and constant desire to search for opportunities and benefit from everything that has been made available to me have their roots in my family's struggle and success in satisfying their hunger for true education. I have been taught to approach school with an eager attitude, pushing myself to face challenges and expanding my knowledge in any way possible.

As a small hint of a smile lingered on his face, I knew that my grandpa did not regret the choices he had made in his life. Through his stories, I came to understand that success comes to those who work diligently and that true satisfaction comes from the knowledge that you have earned your reward. My grandfather's moral resistance in the face of the Communist oppression serves as the anchor to my own value system. He taught me about the inalienability of character and integrity, preparing me for times when my beliefs will be put into question.

Today, my grandpa's place at the kitchen table is empty, and as I begin to pave my journey through life, I am certain that he would be proud to know how he and his stories of courage, perseverance, and self-respect have shaped me into the person I am and the life that I lead.

About the Author: I live in Bellevue, Washington. I have a passion for the biological sciences and wish to pursue a career in public health, as I love helping people and focusing on improving our health system. In my free time, I enjoy playing piano and competing with my father in friendly tennis matches.

High School Attended: International School, Bellevue WA

The Process: I knew that I wanted to write about my family for my Common App essay and how their tough past has influenced me and shaped me into the person that I am today. While writing the essay, I remembered the many times that I talked to my grandfather and the lasting impressions that his stories made on me.

Acknowledgments: First and foremost, I'd like to thank my grandfather, who was the inspiration for my essay. I'd also like to thank my parents, for their perseverance and dedication to overcome the challenges and shortcomings of their youth, and to instill the same values in me.

Irina Duican will be attending The University of California, Berkeley.

WAITING FOR THE STARTING GUN

Danny Eagan

I can spend three hours solving and unsolving a Rubik's cube, watching in satisfaction as one last twist aligns all of the little colored cubes in perfect formation, and then completely mixing it up again only to repeat the process. The next day, I might be sitting on my bed, strumming, picking, and plucking the strings on my guitar, trying diligently to learn a new song, but struggling, because I am my only teacher. The next day I might get up early before school to work out or read a "pleasure book" or write in my journal or play piano, which I also taught myself, or juggle or carve something out of birch or run to school or practice basketball for the upcoming season. And though all my friends tease me about it, completing my homework on a Friday night allows me to erase it from my mind and spend the rest of my sacred weekend bettering myself in another way, shape, or form.

I have learned what passion feels like. I understand its intoxicating presence, the hungry pang it creates deep within, one only satiated by the accomplishment that all of the pain, sweat, early mornings, and late nights offer. In Malcolm Gladwell's book, Outliers, he outlines the idea that to become a true master of a skill, one must dedicate, at minimum, about 10,000 hours to develop and hone it to a level of expertise. I have become enamored with this idea, the basis of which is that with so much passion that I can dedicate the majority of my waking hours to one thing, the practice, repetition, development, and drive towards that one thing will enable me to master it.

As a straight-A student throughout high school thus far while taking some of the most challenging classes our school has to offer, many a time I've received a comment along the lines of "You're so lucky that you're smart, I wish I could get grades like you." But to me, luck has nothing to do with it. Yes, I was raised in a stimulating, supportive environment by my parents, to whom I am eternally grateful, but what most of my peers don't see is the countless late nights, the dents in my pillow from frustrated punches, the time after class spent asking questions to my teachers, that contribute to what they do see. For school, you don't have to love the subject but you have to love to learn. That's where the passion comes in. I would guess that I've logged around 300 hours playing guitar so far, and it has only increased my love for playing the instrument. I haven't loved every second when I was struggling with a certain technique or before my calluses grew in, and it hurt my fingers to play, but the passion that I hold for playing guitar never dimmed and only increased with the constant realizations that there were things on the guitar I couldn't do and that I would have to keep working in order to master them all.

I'm addicted to passion. I want more. I want to explore it, but most of all, I want to find my one thing, my calling. This is my biggest goal: to find something to dedicate myself to and use my initiative and drive to master it, and to use it to better the lives of those around me. Whether it is big or small, I will do it to the best of my ability, and when I find it, my 10,000 hours will begin.

About the Author: I'm a triplet with two sisters and was born and raised in Fairbanks, AK. I enjoy playing guitar, piano, basketball, and running track, and I plan on working with the Peace Corp in a third-world country for a few years after college

High School Attended: Fairbanks, AK (West Valley High School)

The Process: I struggled to come up with a topic that I really cared about for this essay, until my Ms. Heimer asked me "What do you want them [the colleges] to know about you?" I responded that I wanted them to know that I have a lot of passion and dedicate a lot of myself to many different hobbies and projects but really want to find one thing to dedicate myself to. That's where the idea for this essay came from, and I think it provides a nice and provocative glimpse into all of the time, energy, and dedication that I have given to my various pursuits thus far in my life.

Acknowledgments: My AP Literature teacher, Carrie Heimer.

Danny Egan will be attending University of Alaska, Fairbanks.

HOPE FROM TURMOIL

Fadumo Farah

Hand in hand, my mother and my brother came to America in search of hope and answers to prayers. My family originated from Mogadishu, Somalia, where a civil war broke out in 1992. The civil war started out with the collapse of the state and led to clans and warlords fighting for power. Around this time the so-called President of Somali was from a clan by the name of Marexaan, coincidentally the same clan my mother's family is from. The reason behind the state's collapse all boils down to other clans desire to gain power. They believed that it wasn't fair for Marexaans to hold power for almost a decade, so nearly every other clan was fighting for power against each other since the collapse of government. While there was no actual power, Somalis on a daily basis went through the hardship of wondering if they were going to live to see another day.

A typical day consisted of families staying indoors and having the eldest boys and fathers guarding the house from the men of other clans, but the few times one has to go out to gather groceries and produce in order to live are the scariest. In one instance my mother's cousin, by the name of Bilan, a 23-year-old young women went out to get the groceries and, before even making it a block down, encountered men who claimed to be from an opposing clan and violently gang raped her, all the while taking the few amounts of cash she had on her. Learning from a sad mistake, the men of the house vowed to never let their women go through such a cruel situation, so they took it to be their responsibility to get anything that came from outside of the house, whether it was next door, down the block or miles away. One day while a few of the men decided to trek to the next town since food was slowly diminishing from local markets. They left it up to my uncle to guard the girls. Later on as the sun slowly made its way down and the crickets kept to chirping, my uncle drifted from daydreaming to sleeping within a matter of seconds not realizing that he was being watched by a group of drunk men from the opposing clan. The minute the men noticed a normal pattern in his breathing, they ambushed him at gunpoint and proceeded to the house where they found my family. Immediately they demanded all the gold and cash the family had to be put in the sack they carried. My mother's older sister took initiative and claimed that everything they had they sold in return for food, lying, which the men could clearly see through. Sensing the lie, the men threatened to rape each of them in front of my uncle. Frustrated my aunt grabbed her child frantically and asked "Here, in front of my innocent infant?"

On impulse, one of the men snatched her son and tied him and the girls up and advanced towards my aunt and fervently raped her in front of all my family, and as soon as he finished, he untied the family and gave her back her child, remarking "Did it look like he cared?"

Angered, my uncle tried, while the men were preoccupied, to figure out where they put the bag along with their weapons. Noticing that my uncle was preoccupied, the man grabbed his bag encompassing the weapons and aimed a rifle at my uncle's temple. The house was filled with screams and cries, in which my aunt repeatedly kept saying "Not my younger brother, please not him. Take me, take me!" In response, the men fired a bullet that went through her infant son, which she was carrying, killing them both on the spot. This was the day my mother vowed to never let any of her children witness any of the horrid things she had, which the next day they all took refuge to Nairobi, Kenya with few of their belongings.

Knowing my family's struggles, I believe that I can help make a difference in society starting with my education. My family has shaped my dreams and aspirations by giving me the drive I need to understand, no matter what, there will always be somebody that has it worse than me, and I should keep my head high and look at the bigger and brighter picture, also known as my future.

About the Author: My name's Fadumo Farah, I am 17 years old and I currently reside in San Diego, CA. I have hopes and aspirations of studying political science and making a difference slowly and surely in this world.

High School Attended: San Diego, CA

The Process: This essay was very hard for me to write because I had to ask my mom many questions, some of which she wasn't comfortable with because it brought back horrible memories.

Acknowledgments: I would like to acknowledge my parents for molding me into an avid citizen and giving up their life in order for me to have a better one.

MY JOURNEY

Brianna Fedock

Since the age of seven, I knew things were different for me. I knew that my family, if you even called it a family, was different than other families. Since I could remember, my mother and I had always been moving from one place to another, mainly motels, and never staying in one place too long. I knew that this was because my mom could never hold a job for too long, and when she did make money, she would spend it on alcohol or other things that were not necessary. Throughout all these years, my younger sister would visit for some weekends to spend time with my brother and me. Her dad tried his best to make sure that we all still kept in contact and tried to get us to be with each other as much as possible. Eventually, a couple of months passed and my mother had a new boyfriend. This time things were different. We moved into a complex that was semi-permanent. My mother had a son with him.

Every night I prayed my mother would do something different to raise him better than she raised me. Boy was I wrong. It was like I was in flashback mode for the next year and a half. She practically did nothing to raise him. Every day I had to get up at six and get myself ready for school. Throughout this, I also had to take care of my brother, including feed and change him. I would then put him in his play pen and go next door to the neighbor and ask her politely if she could watch my brother for the time being while I was at school. I was barely making it on time to school. When I came home, I would do my homework while trying to make dinner for my younger sibling the best that I could and keeping an eye on him at the same time. This went on until I was the age of ten. By then, I had knew how to cook, clean whatever I could reach, change a diaper, and I knew how to take care of a growing baby. Overall, I knew responsibility at a very young age and learned how to be very dependent on myself.

Sometime during fifth grade, teachers began to question my living situation. I didn't know what to tell them On one hand, I didn't want to get my mother in trouble for her lack of parenting, but on the other hand I didn't want my brother to grow up the way I did. So the truth came out, and my brother and I were taken away from our home. We got separated and put into different child care systems. I did not have contact with my brother for over a year. My sister and her dad always visited me to check up to see how I was doing. Eventually I got out of the Polinsky Center for children, but I didn't go into foster care. I was adopted. I thought it would be scary at first, but when I found out who my adoptive family was, I couldn't have been more ecstatic! I was adopted by my sister's dad. He had been there for me my whole life ever since I could talk, so I considered him my father, even though I didn't know who my real father was. We had gone to court to file the papers. Then it was made official, I finally had a family who would care for me.

As for my brother, he was adopted, too, by a woman who didn't even live in San Diego. I was saddened by this. She made a promise to allow my brother to visit me a lot. That's exactly what they did. To this day, my brother and I remain in contact and see each other quite often. I enjoy my new life and remember that my past made me who I am today. Because I recognized early that my mom, not having a high school diploma, had to move from job to job and struggled financially. I have promised myself throughout this experience, the thing that was running through my mind had been, when I grow up I promised myself that I would go to college, so I can get a good job and be successful and have a family and raise them right. I intend to keep that promise. I want to go to UC to study film to apply the integrity, compassion, and responsibility I learned from the world of my family.

About the Author: My name is Brianna and I live in San Diego, CA. I currently attend the Preuss School UCSD and I am a senior. My goals in life are to become either a director or a producer in the film industry.

High School Attended: The Preuss School UCSD, La Jolla, CA

The Process: rough drafts, teacher meeting, peer editing, revision, final edits, submission.

Acknowledgments: My dad

Some students have a background or story that is so central to their identity that they believe their application would be incomplete without it. If this sounds like you, then please share your story. (Common Application)

IN THE EYES OF A COW

Laura Feigen

I look like a cow.

This is not an overly critical, self-deprecating assessment of my physical appearance. The simple truth is, I painted a self-portrait and it came out resembling a cow. Looking in the mirror, I am a slender soccer-playing enthusiast with dead-set green eyes and large ears (thanks a lot, Grandpa). My unruly, auburn hair twists down like a pack of ravenous snakes, complementing my dark eyebrows whose timid arch makes my stubborn nose and graceful cheekbones ever more prominent. Despite my hopefully human appearance, what should have been a realistic portrait rather resembles a cow-human crossbreed one might unearth from Narnia or Greek mythology. True to my aim, the brushwork and palette composition move to highlight the passionate yet thoughtful character I strive to maintain; however, the calf-like brown skin, muscularly defined shoulders, and slightly turned head give the hapless impression of a Spanish bull about to bulldoze the sparkling matador.

Notwithstanding its cow-like attributes, my self-portrait signifies a critical point in my development as an artist. Raised in a house overflowing with "creative genius," my writer-father and artist-mother continually supported my expressive nature, providing all the macaroni, glue, and crayons my tiny innovative fists could handle. As I matured, my passion for the arts preceded me, and I quickly moved from the modest texture of parent-approved crayon to the more desirably elegant nature of my mother's good pastels, which, much to her displeasure, I frequently used when she ran errands. As the media evolved, so did my subjects and styles. What started out as abstract constructions soon transformed into animals, plants, human figures, and, finally, faces. This last development, and my present state of passion, portraiture, is what defines the cow painting as paramount.

By definition, I am a portrait artist. Manipulating the form of the human face through paint and pastel is a thrill so central to my being that, without it, I am incomplete. Thus, though my self-portrait depicts a woman resembling a cow, I am determined to be content, for not only did its creation help spark my interest in portraiture, but it also reflects the way I experience the world. This portrait highlights an interesting aspect of human nature, or at least, my nature. Specifically, it calls into question our ability to look at things in a completely objective manner and then, hopefully, draw them in a realistic light. Because the reflection we see in the mirror can be very different from the image we would like to present to the public, we subconsciously exchange what our eyes see with what our mind wants. When I'm in the position of deciding how my face will appear on canvas, it is easy to forget that the main point of a self-portrait is to represent your character and air, not by means of accuracy or beauty, but through the materials being used.

Essentially, my art is about preserving imagination. Growing up, like many children, I believed unconditionally in everything wondrous, magical and extraordinary.

Able to conjure up elaborate stories of talking dragons and prince's conquests, I reveled in the typical childhood mindset that couldn't distinguish between reality and fiction. In spite of the fact that I have traded in my macaroni training wheels for my very own set of pastels, I have not lost the ability to believe in the impossible. Like a child, I am still fascinated by the small wonders that life possesses: dappled sunshine through leaves, the ability for sand to stick to everything, and the fact that all food tastes better with Nutella hazelnut spread.

Simply put, I live my life like my cow portrait: filled with imagination, rife with color and rich with emotion. Moo!

About the Author: Born and raised in the Windy City (Chicago, IL), I have always dreamt of traveling the world to examine and explore the artistic traditions of other cultures. At Stanford I desire to double major in cultural anthropology and studio art. Currently, I co-lead a club, "Piece," which strives to better our local community through artistically leaning service endeavors. Recently we finished an 80-foot-long mural for our local train station. To be able to harness the essence of Piece (uniting and beautifying communities) and develop it on a global scale is probably one of my biggest goals in life. In addition to Piece, my extracurriculars include varsity soccer, playing the trumpet, creating tasty, gluten-free pastries and writing/illustrating a book.

High School Attended: Northside College Prep High School, Chicago, IL.

The Process: It took me a while to determine what I wanted to write about for my common application. While brainstorming, I drafted several essays using different prompts and different topics. It was frustrating. Then, one day, I was showing my counselor my art portfolio and she pointed to one of the paintings (my self portrait) and she said: "it kind of looks like a cow." I had always thought this portrait looked like a cow, but I stopped telling people this because it seemed too self critical. However, the more my counselor and I discussed the hilarity of my portrait's appearance, I began to realize that my own perception of my self-portrait was grounded in something much deeper than my literal ability to draw a realistic portrait. Essentially, the unfortunate outcome of this portrait derived from the unique way I viewed the world and, consequently, myself. Because painting has always been an intrinsic part of my personality, I decided to expound upon the perception of my self-portrait and write an essay. Initially, I did not even have a specific essay prompt in mind, I just wrote. Once I had a first draft, I fit it to an essay topic, edited it, and voilà! My common application essay was done.

Acknowledgments: Craig Feigen, Linda Turner, Katherine Mathews, Kiera Doherty, Eleanor Glockner, Leah Schneck, Joel DeLeon, Maxine Freedman, Sophie Leff

Laura Feigen will be attending Stanford University.

FORGIVE

Tarah Fitzgerald

My mother and I greet Joe every Sunday morning as we pass by his office, a tiny security desk at Green-Wood Cemetery. Joe's job is to keep the peace in Green-Wood Cemetery: stop curious bikers, suspicious teens, and exercise junkies from abusing Green-Wood's hidden nooks and calorie-busting hills. Any other security guard would see my mother and me as a threat, suited up with matching green and grey Nikes and an iced coffee each—surely we weren't there for the purpose of mourning. However, Joe just gives us a wink and looks the other way, so off we go for another "soul-purifying power walk" along the 3.5-mile perimeter of Green-Wood Cemetery.

Hollywood blockbusters like Dracula have made graveyards the ghoulish home of vampires and witchcraft. I blame these portrayals for the reluctance of my friends to join me on my walks through Green-Wood. It's hard to believe that in 1838, Green-Wood was as big a tourist attraction as Niagara Falls—families came from all over the city for picnics and carriage rides; now I struggle to wrangle a friend to go in for a quick stroll.

I was once able to persuade a friend to venture along with me under Green-Wood's Gothic arch and onto its enchanting grounds. I was excited to show off the lush flora; however, the cool fall air had already taken its toll on Green-Wood's trees, turning their leaves dull and brittle. I did my best to boast about all of the historic gravestones and exotic mammalia; however, I left the graveyard only fifteen minutes later feeling defeated. It is a difficult task to convince a person, born in a society that teaches you to fear death, to learn to love the physical manifestation of that very thing.

I cannot blame my friends for failing to see Green-Wood's beauty; it was only a few years ago that Green-Wood blossomed for me, as I sat beside Sylvan Pond under a budding cherry tree. I sat alongside my theater group to share personal stories and do some "soul-searching" in preparation for our performance of The Narrator. My fellow actors shared stories of heartbreak and parental disputes; I, however, told a story about my dear friend Sienna, who died from leukemia at the age of seven. It was not a story about my grief, but rather, my cowardice.

I was only ten when Sienna was diagnosed, and I didn't handle her illness well. I avoided her, watching from afar as she grew sicker. The cancer stole her ability to walk; the treatment caused her hair to fall out; and then there was me—who left her without a friend by her side. I was bloated with inner hatred and shame. I had never shared my guilt with anyone before. I was never able to confront the fact that I had acted cowardly. As the details of the story slipped off my tongue, an overwhelming sense of relief came over me.

I remember everything about that day under the cherry tree: the turtles sunbathing along the pond's banks and how everyone blamed the glare off the water for the tears in their eyes, but one thing in particular always stood out upon remembering that day. It was the first time I saw the metallic teal of the Monk parakeet's wings, a native bird to Green-Wood. All the years I had visited, I had never caught sight of these small, majestic creatures until that day under the cherry tree. Its tiny, gray face met mine for a moment before it took off high above Green-Wood's century-old trees.

Every Sunday morning my mother and I walk among the dead. We share stories of those who are remembered, we laugh about the day's events, and we plan for the many years that are to come.

About the Author: My name is Tarah Fitzgerald, and I was born and raised in Brooklyn, NY. I am an aspiring biomedical researcher and hope to someday work for the CDC.

High School Attended: Eleanor Roosevelt High School, NY, NY

The Process: Every day throughout the fall I sat in Green-Wood Cemetery, the focus of my essay, for hours. I kept a journal with me and through the wave of emotions that I felt, reminiscing about the events that inspired my essay, I recorded several thoughts and even some drawings. From my doodling and free-writing, I was able to construct an essay that was both meaningful to me and insightful. After this brainstorming, my essay had its meat and all it needed was some structure and revision. The intense revision process was made possible due to the help of my family, friends, and school officials.

Acknowledgments: Sonia Taitz (college office employee) and my mother, Bernadette Fitzgerald.

Tarah Fitzgerald will be attending the University of Richmond.

THE BIG PICTURE

Julian Fletcher-Taylor

"How would I go about getting a stain off the dining room table?" My brother's question boomed over our car Bluetooth as my parents and I drove home from a camping trip.

"What kind of stain?" asked my mother. "Uh, sodium hydroxide?"

"Sebastian, why were you doing chemistry on the dining room table?" my dad asked in a surprisingly calm tone.

"Well, actually, I was doing an experiment upstairs, but it went through the floor and dropped into downstairs a bit."

Stepping through the door of our house, we could instantly see that "a bit" was an understatement. My brother had dropped a large glass flask as he performed a titration experiment. Glass covered the floor, and the caustic sodium hydroxide solution had burned its way through the bathroom floor and onto the table below, leaving blotchy spots of color. We were just relieved he wasn't badly hurt. From then on, chemistry experiments in our house were done in a lab we made in the basement.

My own science experiments were equally supported. When the first test of my combat robot left a deep gouge in the wall, my parents' response was simply to hand me a can of plaster. My family always found ways to support me in pursuing whatever interested me.

Sitting at that stained table, I learned to love the exchange of ideas. At dinner everyone was always eager to add his or her own view on whatever topic was under discussion at the time. And believe me, an economist, an anthropologist, and a chemistry student are always going to have different perspectives on things. I was the youngest, and, by nature, the quietest, in my family, and at times I felt like I was the least qualified of anyone to speak. Over time, though, I came to love the challenge and learned I had a distinct point of view to contribute.

When I use my telescope to look at the night sky, I have a set of lens filters that enhance specific aspects of an object such as Mars. Orange filters sharpen dust storms, beige helps bring the craters into more detail, and yellow filters sharpen the polar ice caps. Only when each of these views is compiled can you see the entirety of the planet. I see my past eighteen years as a stretch of time when I learned to look through different lenses. From my family I learned that, by listening to different viewpoints around me, I would gain a better understanding of the big picture on almost any topic.

About the Author: My name is Julian Fletcher-Taylor and I live in Berkeley, California. My goals in life are to work on robotics and artificial intelligence and to explore how much these topics can fundamentally change the world.

Describe the world you come from—for example, your family, community or school—and tell us how your world has shaped your dreams and aspirations.

High School Attended: Mentoring Academy, Oakland, California

The Process: My family has helped define the person I am today. It is quirky, interesting, and at times hectic, but my family inspired me to love learning and applying my knowledge to impact the world. I really wanted to write an essay about this, and, after a dozen revisions that attempted to summarize the last 18 amazing years of time with my family, this final version portrays what I will always take with me.

Acknowledgments: I would like to thank Gabrielle Glancy, my family, and John Muster.

Using the statement below as a starting point, tell us about an event or experience that helped you define one of your values or changed how you approach the world.

"Princeton in the Nation's Service" was the title of a speech given by Woodrow Wilson on the 150th anniversary of the University. It became the unofficial Princeton motto and was expanded for the University's 250th anniversary to "Princeton in the nation's service and in the service of all nations." –Woodrow Wilson, Princeton Class of 1879, served on the faculty and was Princeton's president from 1902–1910.

LESSONS IN SERVICE

Maxine Freedman

When I walked up to the podium as an eighth grader at my synagogue to recite Martin Luther King Jr.'s "I Have a Dream" speech, I was crying. The entire sanctuary was silent, probably under the impression that I had been moved to tears by the beauty of Dr. King's words. In truth, I was upset at my rabbi—he was forcing me to stand on two wooden blocks instead of one to recite the speech because I was so small—and, stressed as I was about speaking in front of the entire congregation, it didn't take much for the tears to start.

"Five score years ago . . ." I began feebly. I felt ashamed. Dr. King is one of the greatest organizers of our time and here I was butchering his speech. I told myself to take a deep breath and tried again: ". . . a great American in whose symbolic shadow we stand today . . ." Better. I glanced up at the crowd and my mom smiled at me. I could do this. As I continued, the tears stopped and my voice gained strength. By the end I was practically shouting, and as I finished, people gave me a standing ovation. For one fleeting moment, I felt a spiritual connection to the man who had written this amazing speech.

I am not anywhere near the person that Dr. King was, but that experience marked the beginning of my great admiration for him and my mission to follow his message. This means making a concerted effort to be involved in causes I believe in and to fight for social justice. Since freshman year I have been a part of Mikva Challenge, a citywide organization that works to educate and involve youth in politics. As a member, and now president, of my school's chapter, I have worked for political campaigns with high school students from all over Chicago. During last year's presidential election, I went on a trip to Wisconsin through Mikva Challenge and canvassed to encourage people to vote. I distinctly remember walking up to someone's house, and when we rang the doorbell, a man came walking out from behind the house. "I'm not voting," he blurted out. I faced him, all 5'2" of me, and told him how essential it was that he participate in the political process. He looked surprised, but he took one of our flyers and told us he would go to the early voting rally happening the next day. Even though I cannot verify if he went, his positive response thrilled me and reminded me that it is critical that everyone understands how important s/he is to the political process.

Dr. King has also made a significant impact on my life because of his emphasis on social justice in the context of faith. Social justice is an integral part of Reform Judaism because we believe that tikkun olam, or healing the world, is everyone's responsibility. Whether it's contributing to weekly tzedakah (charity) collection, volunteering to help others learn Hebrew, or participating in my temple's annual mitzvah (good deed) day projects, being an active member of my congregation has always been meaningful to me, even more so since I got the opportunity to read Dr. King's speech. Being involved in Jewish life is so much more than going to religious school or attending services. It means making an active commitment to social justice. That is a commitment I intend to keep.

Princeton's desire to produce civically engaged students resonates with my own goals. I always strive to participate constructively in my community through service or political involvement, whether that community is local, national, or international. Being involved with Princeton's Community Based Learning Initiative and other similar programs will allow me to broaden my perspectives and grow into the active citizen I have worked to be since I stepped down from my temple's podium four years ago.

About the Author: I'm a 17-year-old Jewish girl from Chicago, Illinois. My goal in life is to work in diplomacy in an effort to find a peaceful solution for the world's problems.

High School Attended: Northside College Preparatory High School, Chicago, Illinois

The Process: To write this essay I started thinking about when I really began to feel motivated to take part in community service and social justice activities. I was also inspired by the connection between these activities and faith. When I first wrote the essay, I tried cramming in everything I possibly could about work I had done with Mikva Challenge and at my temple. Upon rewriting the essay, I worked to streamline my thoughts so that it was the larger idea of being in the nation's service that came through rather than random events I had taken part in.

Acknowledgments: Audrey Stillerman, Linda Turner, Aggie Stewart

Maxine Freedman will be attending Macalester College.

HOME

Nicolette Guida

Close your eyes and imagine this: walking into a room and suddenly being whisked away by a melody of deliciously beautiful aromas. Your mouth begins to water, but there isn't much time to dwell on the saliva dripping down the corners of your mouth because you hear a tune that distracts you, shifting your focus to something slightly more pleasant. The incessant beat fills up your ears and spills over into your soul, making you excited, anxious, and a little bit hungry all at the same time. The knives chop steadily on the cutting board, keeping the beat. The pots and pans join in, clanging away and the forks and spoons add the most delicate clink. Upon the stove the boiling water bubbles and the meatballs sizzle. This is my kitchen where my family is busy at work preparing dinner. In tune with an old Italian tradition my family gathers together each Sunday for dinner. Despite our whirlwind lives during the week, complete with hectic schedules and personal issues, come Sunday, no matter where we are or what we're doing we leave our worries at the door and gather around the table to share food, laughter and quality time with one another.

As picturesque as this may seem to the outside world, it is not a five star restaurant. The degree of formality here is nonexistent. It all begins with the preparation period, when all of the actual cooking takes place, and when I seemingly bubble over with anticipation. My stomach grumbles and roars with the ferocity of a prowling jungle cat. The gurgling is so embarrassingly loud it makes me glad that I am, in fact, at home and not at a lavish feast, where at this point I would probably have to crawl under the table in complete ignominy. Once the cutlets are baked, the meatballs are fried, the bread is toasted, and, of course, the pasta is "al dente," it is officially dinnertime. Plates and utensils are passed with lightning speed and fly to their positions. As the food hits the surface of the table, flocks of people swarm in with the same ceaseless, ravishing hunger as that of relentless seagulls. This is where the real action happens. Voices compete over one another, hands grab, arms stretch, and bodies are practically slung over the table in an undying effort to grab that last bit of Italian bread at the farthest corner of the table. I can barely hear myself think amongst the requests to "please pass the grated cheese" and the not so polite "give me more pasta now." Amidst all the activity, my grandma attempts to furtively sneak a taste of chicken parmesan without using the designated serving utensil; however, her efforts are squelched when my germ-phobic and, apparently, very observant aunt starts to scold her thus prompting the entire table to once again erupt in conversation.

Sitting at the table, I take a look at the smiling, warm and familiar faces that surround me. They're loud, they're hungry, and sometimes they can be a bit obnoxious, but at the end of the day they're my family and I love them. I find comfort in the presence of my family and the giant serving of carbohydrates doused in fresh tomato sauce. I don't have to wear a mask or pretend to be someone I'm not. I'm stripped down to the essence of my true self, which is ridden with imperfections, but it doesn't matter because I know that my family will accept and approve of me no matter what. I don't need the finest things in life to be happy, I have everything I need right here. Here, where I can grab my food. Here, where I can be myself. Here, where I am surrounded by those who will love me unconditionally and annoy me interminably. Here, where I am home.

About the Author: My name is Nicolette Guida, I am 17 years old, and I live in Staten Island, New York. My goal is to further my education and broaden my academic and social horizons by attending college.

High School Attended: Staten Island Technical High School, Staten Island, NY

The Process: The essay prompt directed me to write about the place where I felt most content. I had a lot of ideas about what to write about, but it didn't take me too long to pinpoint the exact spot where I am most happy and content. That spot is at my kitchen table surrounded by the familiar and loving faces of my family. After I committed myself to a topic, I wrote a rough draft and edited the essay until it was as close to perfect as it could possibly be. I also had it read and critiqued by my parents, my teachers and some of my peers.

Acknowledgments: Thank you, Mom, for all your help and support.

Nicolette Guida will be attending Macaulay Honors College at CSI.

WAR, VIOLENCE, BLOODSHED . . .

Asha Haghi

were the last images I saw of my poverty-stricken home country before I boarded the plane. It was 1998 and my home country, Kenya, was deeply affected by the civil war that broke out in Somalia. The only way to stay alive, through my mother's eyes, was to flee. My courageous, single mother made the brave decision to take her two young girls, while pregnant with a third, and leave Kenya for the United States. Growing up, my mother was cheated of the simple privileges of easy access to food, a comfortable, safe home, and an education. Barely graduating from high school, my mother's mission was to build a brighter future for her daughters.

As we flew closer and closer towards the beautiful skies of San Diego I grasped my mother's hand and looked into her beautiful eyes, and I saw the light of a new life. We resided in San Diego, California because my mother had family there. Once we arrived, obstacles and challenges loomed over our heads. My mother had to find a job and enter her young children in a local school. My mother somehow found a way to leap over each obstacle and confront each challenge presented to her. A single mother with a five-year-old, three-year-old, and a newborn child was a struggle, but my mother continued to work hard and strive to provide the life she never had for her daughters.

Although my older sister and I were born in Kenya, our family is from a Somali background. Growing up in a Somalian community, I learned that in order to be successful I must gain an education and never be ashamed of where I come from. Witnessing Somali immigrant mothers, including my own, struggling to put food on the table really opened my eyes to the fact that education means opportunity in the US. I have made it my mission to gain an education and become successful. I want to make my mother proud and put to good use all the sacrifices she made for her children. With the opportunities she granted me, I am now able to obtain a college education. I also want to pursue a higher education for myself because I love the thrill of learning new things, and I look forward to using the education I gain to make a difference in the world.

Since the moment I entered school, I knew that I had to work hard and strive to be nothing but the best. Attending the Preuss School UCSD, I faced many challenges such as long bus rides and countless sleepless nights studying. I overcame most of these challenges by being grateful for my life in America and reminiscing about where would I have been if I never left Kenya. If it were not for the education I have acquired through the past fourteen years, my life would have been completely different. Anytime I feel too tired to study for that advanced placement exam, my mother's support and encouragement fuels me to study hard for a couple more hours. The reaction on my mother's face when she saw my A+ in math showed me that she was proud of my accomplishments. Her happiness gave me a sense of fulfillment that I am able to make my mother proud.

The sacrifices that my mother made for my sisters and me influenced me to continue to pursue a higher education. After I graduate from the Preuss School UCSD, I plan to attend the University of California. I am interested in pursing a bachelor's degree in business. I hope to create my own company helping young immigrant kids pursue an education and become successful. For all my successes in life, I am thankful for my hardworking mother who created a bright future for her daughters. Through education, I am creating that future.

About the Author: My name is Asha Haghi, I am currently living in San Diego, California, but am originally from Kenya. My goals in life include graduating high school, attending a four-year university, and making a living in order to financially assist my single mother.

High School Attended: Preuss School UCSD, La Jolla, CA

The Process: I first brainstormed, then took time writing the essays, had a few people edit for me, then I fixed the corrections.

Acknowledgments: I would like to acknowledge my English teacher, Ms. Gabay, for editing the essay; my older sister Fatima for editing the essay as well; and my mother for inspiring my essay.

The Admissions Committee would like to learn why you are a good fit for your undergraduate school choice (College of Arts and Sciences, School of Nursing, The Wharton School, or Penn Engineering). Please tell us about specific academic, service, and/or research opportunities at the University of Pennsylvania that resonate with your background, interests, and goals.

MUSINGS ON A
CAMPUS TOUR

Anna Hess

The wet rain and thick cloud cover over Philadelphia blocked out the sun on a classic east coast day at Penn. Looking up at the grayness through the trees scattered across the green, I abandoned my family to wander aimlessly and bask in the weather. (You know those SoCal kids that find perfect sunny days to be so monotonous? Guilty as charged.) I ambled along the walkway in front of College Hall, and my geeky love for American history promptly had me obsessing over the year 1876 printed on its sign. I imagined the Second Industrial Revolution sweeping across the US, Reconstruction coming to a close, and captains of industry rising to power as policy wonk students just like me debated robber barons in this very spot. Each century-old Ivy Day carving etched onto the façade of the building felt rough under my fingertips and drew me more and more into the magic of this place.

Once I tore myself from the hall, I strolled past the rust-colored Fisher Library only to be stopped by a Penn junior with chalk smeared all over his face. He was surrounded by supportive messages scrawled onto the red brick, all meant to erase the stigma of being mentally disabled. Before I knew it, he had me on my hands and knees etching "Everyone is unique" in green chalk onto the damp path. I thought of Kristina back in L.A., my friend with microcephaly who I tutor in reading each Monday, and I saw the bright smile I knew she'd wear if only she were here to see this. Everything I had heard about the Penn Civic House was here in action right in front of me—and I could get used to this.

Next stop was Bennett Hall, where I would fall in love with Penn's Cinema Studies program. My father (Class of '84) raised our family to adore film: Through elementary and middle school, Sunday night was black-and-white movie night, where Ginger Rogers and Gene Kelly danced across the screen. We had Netflix back when it was just a DVD delivery service, years before it streamed online and dominated the Emmys. I've taken film classes since sixth grade and have a countless number of extraordinarily amateur shorts I made at middle-school filmmaking camps hidden in the depths of my computer. (If you ever asked to see them, I would regretfully decline.) I've had my best days working on film sets as a lackey delivering fruit salads to stars, and I've loved every minute of my film upbringing—Penn Cinema Studies is exactly where all my fun-and-games could mutate into a career.

While I marveled at the department's archives, I heard all about the program from its passionate administrators. Director Decherney's and Professor Gentili's words confirmed that my infatuation with film could be cultivated here, and that this tight-knit community is exactly where I need to be. Each course speaks to every side of me: the eight international film courses to my obsession with travel, cinema & globalization to my journalist's eye on society, and the documentary film classes to my fixation on change-inspiring filmmaking.

At the end of the day, once my dad had finally succeeded in prying me off campus, I spent the entire rental car ride down a gridlocked I-76 demanding absolute silence while I dissected the Daily Pennsylvanian.

Would I one day take part in the Econ Scream? How did they get Tyga to perform at Spring Fling '13? I compared my school's paper to the DP— the keen eyes of these editor-in-chiefs made my editing and reporting seem kind of unfortunate. But one thing was for sure: If I were given the chance, I'd bring everything I've got to this editorial team.

By the time my airplane home abruptly touched down at LAX, I knew that I could never imagine myself anywhere but Penn.

About the Author: I am Anna Hess from Los Angeles, CA, currently attending Crossroads School in Santa Monica. I have been accepted Early Decision to the School of Arts and Sciences at the University of Pennsylvania and plan on majoring in philosophy, politics, and economics (PPE) as a pre-law track. After receiving my undergraduate and law degrees, my dream is to be a broadcast journalist that covers legal beats, using a background in jurisprudence to report with insight.

High School Attended: Crossroads School for the Arts and Sciences, Santa Monica, CA

The Process: I began writing this supplemental essay in August 2013 for an October 2013 Early Decision deadline. I cycled through three distinctly different drafts of this essay. I wrote the first before I visited the University of Pennsylvania campus, the second after I visited in August, and the final third after I visited again in early October. These visits vitally shaped my final draft as it walks the reader through my experience on the campus tour.

Acknowledgments: Rick Hess (Father)

Anna Hess will be attending The University of Pennsylvania.

THE JOURNEY TO COLLEGE

Ali Ibrahim

In 1991 in the midst of a very horrific and brutal war, my parents fled Somalia seeking refuge in neighboring Kenya. As the country plunged into civil war, peace and stability were quickly replaced with violence and desperation, which would markedly change the country for over twenty years. My family experienced the horror overnight as gun shots rang through the once quiet seaside capital, as smoke and debris from burned houses filled the air. To make things worse, the country was struck by a severe drought causing great famine. I was born five years later in one of the largest refugee camps, and the experience of living there for eight years, until we arrived safely in San Diego in 2004, changed who I am today and who I want to be in future. These camps only consisted of tents or mud houses and few basic supplies, but it meant the world to my family. It meant that we got to escape the war and all the violence that came with it; it meant that I also got the medical aid that helped me overcome tuberculosis, which claimed so many other kids like me.

Moving to the US represented a second chance at life for my family. Upon our arrival, my parents knew they would no longer have the fear of violence and uncertainty but could return to focusing on our future. We regained the hope to live, to dream, and to get through every day striving to succeed in safety. I neither shame nor dwell on the agonizing past because I am too busy dreaming of and working hard for a brighter future. My family's collective past leaves a burning desire within my heart to be a better person every day so our struggles do not go in vain. This has been the beacon of my motivation as I stay after school for activities like robotics clubs and helping myself and my peers to aim higher and develop new talents. It is why I got involved to coach a First Lego League team and try to help younger students build an enduring interest in science and technology.

I plan on using my past to power me through the University of California because I know that getting an engineering degree is not easy, especially since my two older siblings dropped out of high school, making me family flag bearer. I want to major in electrical engineering and computer science because it is both what I am good at academically and enjoy practically. This decision has been long in the making since when I was in 9th grade reading about great achievers like Elon Musk and Steve Jobs. I love to program and crave the chance to master it in college. I look forward to programming and building things on a daily basis at the University of California and plan on carrying the story of my past as a catalyst for my growth rather than as a hindrance.

About the Author: I live in San Diego, CA. I plan on majoring in electrical engineering and computer science.

High School Attended: The Preuss School UCSD, La Jolla, CA

The Process: I wrote the essay. I had my English teacher look over it, fixed the mistakes, and follow her advice that I agreed with. Had my art teacher edit it. Fixed the mistakes again. I then let my family look over it and then had my advisory teacher look over it.

Acknowledgments: Advisory teacher, English teacher, art teacher, and family.

Ali Ibrahim will be attending UCSD.

CHERUBINO'S GIFT

Julia Joo

Cherubino trembled in anticipation. He felt the eyes of his audience members, and deep inside he was terrified. But there was no time to waste on such trivialities. Despite the butterflies in his stomach, he needed to tell her how he felt.

He nodded toward the piano.

Immediately, the entire hall reverberated with the signature staccato chords of Mozart's aria, "Voi Che Sapete." The enamored young boy took a few steps closer to his dazzling beloved at the far end of the room, eager to profess the tempest of his emotions in a passionate soliloquy to his first love.

As he began to sing, the boy became a man, exposing in his powerful soprano everything from the ineffable lightness of heart to the fiery fits of pain that unrelentingly beset his chest. As his lover expressed signs of disinterest in his fervent confession, Cherubino became even more emphatic. He begged the silent figures before him to explain the chaos of his uncontrollable emotions one last time before clasping his hands together in silence. After the piano's last chord, the theater was deafeningly silent. Then the hall erupted with applause.

The setting, no longer the magnificently gilded boudoir of a lavish Spanish palace, was once again the dreary school auditorium. Where Cherubino had stood so love-stricken on the stage, a petite Korean girl appeared, still shaking with undrained adrenaline but no longer the nervous wreck she had been before her performance. Cherubino's love interest at the back wall was once again just a nick in the concrete. I was barely able to stand; my fingers, head, and toes throbbed heavily. But I loved all of it. I wanted to stay there—basking in the love of the crowd, the warmth of the spotlight, the glory of success, the height of my confidence—forever.

Snapping out of my reverie, I sought my father in the audience. This had been his first time seeing me perform on stage. I burst into a smile, winking away my tears, when I spotted him, furiously snapping away on the camera. When he noticed me looking, he stood up and placed the camera on his seat. After quickly wiping his eyes on his sleeve, he began to cheer with an uncharacteristic vigor. As my eyes swept over the rest of the crowd, my chest swelled to see the mouths of my peers gaping open. Was this beaming young woman really the same girl who always kept to herself during Music Honor Society meetings? The woman who did not even muster a word when she so hesitatingly raised her hand to sign up to perform tonight?

This might have been my thirtieth time on the stage, but the first twenty-nine performances had been spent as a violinist. As a violinist, I had never felt powerful on stage; I had never received a standing ovation, never brought my father to tears. Even so, I had felt like I had lost half of my life when I had to give my instrument of ten years up to the recession. But today, having found my real musical passion, I did not feel so sad anymore.

After the applause finally died down and I ran down the stairs into my father's warm embrace, I was grateful to Cherubino for showing me the thrill of being the center of attention. Today, faced with intimidatingly high expectations, I had needed him to gather my courage. But tomorrow, I knew I would not have to hide behind a character to express myself.

About the Author: I attend International School in Bellevue, Washington. I intend on becoming a pediatrician to help realize my passion for serving as a bulwark for immigrant families like mine against the consequences of cultural barriers in the field of medicine.

The Process: One of the greatest experiences that had a significant impact on my character is my love for singing and performing. Receiving a standing ovation from the audience after my first solo vocal performance gave me a fantastic boost in confidence and fervor for performing on stage. I realized that writing an essay about this experience would give colleges a better context for my extracurricular leadership roles and provide a new perspective of myself as a girl who loves music rather than simply as a prospective matriculate.

Acknowledgments: My older sister played a significant role in helping me fine-tune this essay.

INTERCONNECTEDNESS

Zoe Kamil

For as long as I can remember, I've loved cities—and the people who live in them. I think it began when I was in elementary school, and I went to school on the opposite side of San Francisco from where I lived. Every morning, we drove through multitudes of colorful neighborhoods, and I listened to the early morning noises of its dwellers, imagining the lives they led and making up stories about them.

Though I no longer make that particular cross-city trek, its lasting effects are apparent in my life. To this day, as I'm making my way through the city, hopping from bus to crowded bus, I can't help imagining the lives of the people around me. Perhaps the tired-looking woman with the squealing baby has secret dreams of being a concert cellist. Maybe the smiling man sitting beside me is on his way to propose to his girlfriend or boyfriend.

I firmly believe that every time I step out in to the world, the people, and places, and moments I observe find their way into my artistic works, sometimes consciously, sometimes not. I've written plays based on surprising interactions, adventures in San Francisco's wackiest neighborhoods, and snippets of lovers' quarrels overheard on the Highline in New York City. I've built characters around mannerisms that I've noticed in the behavior of my friends and family. To put it simply: The art I create is inspired by diversity and the often-absurd nature of everyday life.

When I tell people that I want to live and pursue theatre production in New York City, I generally expect one of two responses. The first one is less than enthusiastic: "Oh, how could you want to live there? There's so much going on all the time! And it's so overwhelming . . . so competitive." The second is usually marked by a wide, knowing grin and a sparkle in the eyes: "That's such a magical place." Those are the people that understand what its like to feel a desperate, driving force to belong to something huge and to be part of a wild rhythm of passion and noise and the sense of extended community that can only come from geographical closeness.

For as long as I can remember, I've had that force inside of myself, and I consider it to be one of my greatest and most distinguishing characteristics as an artist. I never feel more inspired than when I'm navigating the pavement of a crowded street, at once entirely anonymous and very much a part of something huge. If I've learned one thing about myself in my life so far, it's that I'm at my happiest when I feel connected to the world, and I feel most connected to the world when I'm writing, doing, and immersing myself in theatre.

About the Author: My name is Zoe Kamil, and I live in San Francisco, CA. For as long as I can remember, I've wanted to pursue a career in the theatrical realm—as a director, playwright, producer, and performer.

High School Attended: Jewish Community High School of the Bay, San Francisco, California

The Process: When it came time for me to write my college essays, I found them coming easily to me, because I was so passionate about what I was writing about. This one in particular truly seemed to flow out of me. With my mom's help, I tightened it up a bit, and the second draft became the one I submitted.

Acknowledgments: My mother

Zoe Kamil will be attending Marymount Manhattan College.

AIM HIGH

Zoey Maleekah LaChance

I come from a long line of short, strong women. Our average height is about five feet, but what we lack in altitude, we make up for in attitude. I have been taught to be proud of my stature, to embrace it, but just like people who are considered too fat or too tall or too curvy, we petites get put down because of our body type. The short kid in the corner with her head immersed in a chapter book is an easy target for those children who are bored in school. Add in the fact that I had just moved into town the day before school started in first grade, and I was prime bait. However, there are times during a fishing trip when the bait gets away, dropped on the ground from a first time fisherman's clumsy, shaking hands. My fisherman's name was History. With History, I could escape in a covered wagon, bumping along the dusty Oregon Trail to new lands. With History, I could wear dresses with high collars and buy wrapped jewels of penny candy at the corner store. With History, I could be a cowboy even though my great-great-great-great grandmother was an American Indian. The Western Expansion was my getaway, and, looking back, a little bit of my obsession. I read every book I could, knew every fact, and by third grade, I was even dressing like a cowgirl. I had the whole getup: boots, hat, dress, and belt. I still have them all in my closet. So, that Halloween day, I wore them to school. My teacher took one look at me and rushed quick as a whisper, to the bookcase, a puckish smile lighting up his face. Still smiling, he handed me a thin book. I looked down to see a plain woman in a cowboy hat, her face peaceful and brave. This was how I met Annie Oakley. Not the Annie Oakley that everybody knows, the one

who is loud, sexy, and Western, but the real Annie Oakley: quiet, de-
mure, and Ohioan. Despite her humble background, she was one of the
premier sharpshooters of her time, and although I have never picked up a
gun, I felt a sense of kinship with her. That's when I learned: Annie Oakley, the real Annie Oakley, was only five feet tall, the same height that I
am now! Knowing that she went through the same experience as I did in
being teased for her height and, as a performer, being told that she was
too small to do what she loved, inspired me. We proved our skeptics
wrong, the two of us, her bravery spurring mine even today. Because she
did not quit, I did not quit, and now I am proud to be the same height
as her. Annie Oakley said "Aim at a high mark and you will hit it." So, I
aim high in everything I do. Even higher than I can reach.

About the Author: My name is Zoey Maleekah LaChance, and I live in Williston, Vermont, surrounded by trees and mountains. My goals in life are varied and multidimensional, but my main goal is to move to Stratford-upon-Avon in England and become a professional Shakespeare scholar.

High School Attended: Champlain Valley Union High School, Hinesburg, Vermont

The Process: My father, an English teacher, encouraged me to write my college essay early, in the summer before my junior year. My father advised me not to attempt writing an essay based on the Common Application prompt about describing a person who had in impact on your life because he had never known a student who had successfully pulled it off. Always one for a challenge, I wrote my essay based on that prompt anyway. I edited my essay several times until I thought it showcased me in a personal and unique way. The Common Application prompts have since changed, but my essay was still applicable because I put so much of my personal story into it.

Acknowledgments: My father, Marc-Andre LaChance; college counselor, Nancy Milne; and my 3rd grade teacher, Mr. David Bouchard, for introducing me to my hero.

Zoey Maleekah LaChance will be attending Drew University.

MY PERSONAL STRUGGLE

Lisa Le

I am the child of a mother who works hard to support her three children as well as herself. My parents got a divorce when I was young, around the age of six, and that was when my life became even more difficult than I ever imagined. The night that my parents fought, the police took my brother, my sister, and me away to a place called "Polinsky Children's Center," a temporary emergency shelter for children. I was so scared and I did not know what was going on. I lived there for months and was separated from my brother and sister. When I found out I was finally able to leave and live with my grandparents, my dad's parents, I found out that only my brother could come with me and not my sister. Since my sister is my half sister and not related to my dad, she was not allowed to come live with my brother and me. She had to stay behind and eventually got adopted into another family.

When I was in elementary school, the court decided that my dad was legally not allowed to see me or my siblings. Every day my grandpa walked me to school while my grandma stayed home and took care of my brother. They became my second parents. After living with my grandparents for a year, the court allowed my brother and me to move back in with my mom. At home my mom was struggling to take care of two kids by herself, so I had to help my mom any way I could. I took care of my brother, cleaned around our home, and made sure my brother and I ate while my mom worked endless nights so she could try to take care of us. At one point my brother and I had to live at our friend's house so my mom could work. I only got to see her on the weekends.

When she stopped working late nights, my mom and I fought about almost everything. I did not know the tension within the house would become so bad.

To deal with everything that was going on at home, I decided to focus more in school. Every day I had to speak to a social worker at school. Whenever my mom and I fought, I was so thankful that school was there to be my break from all my issues at home. I gained strong relationships with my teachers who helped me through all the issues I was having at home. When I got into the Preuss UCSD, the tension between my mom and me got worse because now I had more work to deal with from school as well as the arguments that seemed to get worse. The tension suddenly stopped during my junior year.

During my junior year my mom was diagnosed with thyroid cancer. My mom and I were emotional wrecks. After we found out that my mom had cancer, it was just one doctor's visit after another trying to figure out a plan for her treatment. All the visits took a toll on me and my school work, but helped me. I figured out what I wanted to do with my future.

I set goals for myself, and those goals are to get into college, get a degree in biochemistry, then focus my future on cancer research. I never realized how emotionally painful it would be to figure out that my mom had a sickness that could potentially kill her. Therefore my mom inspired me to want to spend my future trying to help find a cure for cancer, and she has helped me realize how important it is to have a relationship with my family and spend time with before we all leave to go on with our individual lives in the future.

About the Author: My name is Lisa Le, I am 17 years old, and I am born and raised in San Diego. My goal in life to major in biochemistry and eventually work in the cancer researching field.

High School Attended: The Preuss School UCSD, La Jolla CA

The Process: The Preuss School UCSD, La Jolla CA

Acknowledgments: Mom and my teachers

Lisa Le will be attending Cal State University East Bay.

THE GEEKS SHALL
INHERIT THE UNIVERSE

Amanda Lee

Celebrate your Nerdy Side!

I proudly self-identify as a nerd or a geek. Now, others can think otherwise, but I think I got the qualities. I laugh at XKCD. I'm subscribed to YouTube channels like Vsauce, Mental Floss, and SciShow. I stay home on Friday nights doing homework because it's better than the imaginary parties I get invited to. I've gone LARPing before, I quote Monty Python, and, yes, I did write a Star Wars-themed common app essay. From knowing the nuances in of each style of EDM to staying up until midnight roleplaying, I would say I have many nerdy qualities.

But when someone tells me to celebrate being a nerd, it's more than getting really enthusiastic about a topic. Nerds and geeks share a common thread. It starts with a discovery. This experience leads to an attachment, and then comes an understanding. It's knowing how excited someone gets when they are allowed to geek out or how gratifying a nerd feels when someone laughs at their awkwardly executed programming joke, pun intended. That's what makes being nerdy so awesome; there is that empathy that connects us, even if we don't love the same subjects. It may be weird, uncool, or "nerdy," but that doesn't matter when you're passionate. Let your freak flag fly because, no matter what they say, celebrating the power of human intellect, curiosity, and excitement, is awesome. Power to the nerds and the geeks, and don't forget to be awesome.

About the Author: My name is Amanda Lee. Apart from the homework I do every day in my large house-haven in the beautiful land of Colorado, I am a nerd. My life goals include mastering the art of college-ing, staring at penguins, publishing a piece of literature, and solving the diaper-garbage crisis.

High School Attended: Peak to Peak Charter School, Lafayette, Colorado

The Process: This actually became one of the reasons I applied to Tufts. I had been looking at the university because of its eclectic-ness, but this sealed the deal. Applicants had to chose from six essays, and even though responding to Virginia Woolf and talking about #YOLO seemed very enticing, "celebrating one's nerdy side" excited me the most. Since I am a little bit nerdy, this essay ended up being the easiest essay to write. I basically took the fun parts of my life and synthesized it into a paragraph.

That being said, because I am part of the Nerdfighter fan-base, John Green's exposé on being a nerd really echoed with what I wanted to bring across. Due to the communities I've grown up in, I've never been bullied for being unabashedly enthusiastic about EDM music or roleplaying, but I have definitely seen people ridiculed for drawing or identifying with particular fandoms, like Twilight or One Direction. Seeing what people have gone through as well as marveling at what my friends do pushed me to write about what nerdiness and geekery mean in a greater context.

Acknowledgments: Thank you, Mrs. Kristie Letter, my English teacher; Mrs. Linda Bostic, my counselor; my second mother, Meg Lineham; and, of course, my amazing mom. Without you guys, I would probably be living in my room, watching Adventure Time and getting really fat. I would also like to thank Ms. Carla Flanhofer and Mr. Kurt Schaefer for writing my letters of rec and convincing me that I am good enough for college.

Amanda Lee will be attending Swarthmore College.

TAKING A RISK

Andrew Lee

I looked down at my hands. Although the room was dark, I saw the perspiration gathering in my palms. Feeling the sweat pulsating from my pores, I squirmed in discomfort. Deep in thought, I jolted back to reality when I heard the booming crack of a gunshot. Low, menacing, baseheavy music filled my ears, and for a moment, I was enticed by a different distraction. This was only a transient diversion, because I soon remembered where I was and why I was there. There was a more important matter at hand; I could not risk being distracted by a silly cop chase.

I felt my heart pounding. Surely everyone around me could hear it. I felt exposed and stared at. Luckily, it was still dark. Nobody noticed my presence; I was still in control of the situation. Once again, I stared down at where my hands were. I looked around and checked to make sure nobody was watching. I started to make my move, but BOOM, another gunshot, and I had to retreat deeper into my seated position.

I sniffed the air. There was a pervasive salty scent that was noxious. Maybe it was popcorn; hopefully it was not my body odor. I started to wonder if my movements would be detected as a result of the emanating odor from my body, but I was calmed by a purple smell. The arousing aroma was sweet, yet it did not drown the air with its scent. Somehow I knew that achieving my objective would reward me with more of this mesmerizing waft of beauty.

I heard the time ticking by. The cop chase had ended and conflicts were resolving; yet, I was still motionless, stuck in a deep dilemma—to pounce, or to remain stationary—for my mission had not yet been accomplished. I looked over at my objective and stared. It was right there —ready for me to take and grasp. I had to make a decision. I had to act fast. But, I still needed poise, composure; I couldn't risk rushing things.

I could taste the imminent glory. I knew I had to act. My heart told me to. If I couldn't get myself to reach out, the regret would consume my conscience and pester me for eternity. "It will be worth it," I told myself, "This is what you need to do."

I knew I wanted to, and I knew this golden opportunity would never present itself again. So, I summoned all the courage I could muster. I couldn't just sit there. I couldn't be passive. Failure was not an option. Extending my hand, before it was too late, I slowly but surely reached over, ever so slightly, and held her hand, for the rest of the movie, until the credits.

About the Author: My name is Andrew Lee and I am from the Seattle suburbs of Bellevue, WA. In college, I hope to be able to explore my passions for mathematics and social sciences. As for the rest of my life beyond college, my goal is to live a life where I can be myself and enjoy what I do.

High School Attended: International School, Bellevue, WA

The Process: Just have fun and write. Enjoy yourself. Write in a "This is me" mindset, and don't make any compromises. Just go for it and hopefully there will be a school that clicks with your voice and style.

Acknowledgements: Guidance counselor, for always helping with the college process. Parents, for always supporting me in times of stress. Friends, for giving me the positive feedback to encourage me to have fun with my writing.

Andrew Lee will be attending Washington University in St. Louis.

BREAKING REALITY

Jun Lee
— Second Place

As soon as I walk through the rusty, double doors of the gym, the dull ringing of the last bell of school fades away into the distance and my lips form a wide grin as I race up the bright stairs into the small vacant room on the second floor of the gym. Past the door, I'm met with the beautiful and familiar breeze of sweat, shoes, and body odor along with the vibrant colors of 80s funk blasting from the radio. The muffled music now comes to life, the bass line synchronizing in tune with my heartbeat as I place my backpack down, the thrill and bliss of the upbeat tune rushing into my body. In an instant, I become one with the music. My body takes over; it speaks for me, announcing my entrance as my feet and my hands paint a picture of the floor, flowing and twisting in harmony with the melodies, my feet squeaking from the friction with the ground and my hands burning from the pressure as my body ends up on a one-hand handstand as the music reaches its climax. I am met with whoops and yells from my fellow brothers and sisters as my feet land back on the floor of my second home, the Breakdance Club.

Although barely big enough to fit us all, this rare club is what I look forward to every Tuesday and Thursday after school, a place unknown to the mass of students, a place that invites individuality and rewards creativity. The club embodies a comfortable zone where I can leave all of my worries and stress about life at the front door and simply create an enjoyable perspective about my rigorous academic life through a hobby that I love. On the floor, I can solve my physics homework physically, completing calculations in a whiz as I befriend gravity mid-air, redefining motion and displacement in real time as my body spins upon the floor, experiencing instantaneous acceleration like none other. Transferring my momentum, I can thrust my body into a freeze and stop time briefly—long enough to take a short gasp—and land back onto my feet to the world spinning in circular motions. Calculus becomes a breeze as my body embodies a function, the notes in the background plotting graphs, axes, and points as I weave through them, bound by limitless chains of infinity. Unlike a mundane classroom, Breakdance Club offers for me an extraordinary community of fellowship and intellectual productivity, each of us thriving to contribute a new move or interpretation. Bouncing off each other's ideas, showing off our best and worst techniques comfortably and equally, we learn from criticism and embrace each other through the physical and mental stress without judgment. Most importantly, we are able to look at life through a different lens. To the bystanders, I am merely moving my body; to me, I am viewing the world in a different dimension. In reality, I discover originality in the art of dance. Physics, calculus, and life—all are all topics I can explore through physical expression, to find that they are all interconnected seamlessly. In many ways, my entity serves as a living example of the concepts I learn in school.

Consequently, dance becomes a tangible and palpable gateway into the realm of dreams and innovations. Others view the dance as excruciating, extreme, and difficult, but to me, pain and discomfort are not ramifications but rather, indicators and milestones of accomplishment. Indeed, breakdance is an art that welcomes bruises, sweat, and failure, combining all to engender a performance and a unique form of choreography to which none can compare.

About the Author: My name is Jun Lee, I live in Tucson, Arizona

My goals in life are to pursue and strive for what I love to do and achieve higher levels of education; to always work with diligence and passion, innovating, growing, learning in order to teach and help those around me and make the world a more productive and happier place.

High School Attended: Tucson, AZ, University High School

The Process: Essentially, I found something I loved doing (breakdance) and wrote about my feelings and relationship to it, along with how such a hobby connected on a more daily and personal aspect.

With the idea inspired and solidified, the details and flow came naturally; sure, I had many teachers and friends read over the essay and offer criticisms and their own opinions, but to me the essay was truly born through a long period of thought and reflection in the privacy of my room and during long showers. Although the outside assistance was pivotal, the essay mostly took a lot of thinking and meditation rather than writing and editing.

Acknowledgments: I'd like to thank my family and my English teacher (Mrs. Tully) for supporting me and always encouraging me to strive for more.

Jun Lee will be attending The University of Arizona.

Describe the world you come from—for example, your family, community or school—and tell us how your world has shaped your dreams and aspirations. (University of California)

MY COLLECTIVE BAD

Kevin Lee

This World does not sleep. It blossoms with people and technology and romance and I sample its petals.

This World feeds off of desire. It gorges itself full of greed and lust and sin and I take it all in.

This World is full of tragedy. I witness and live in This World that tears itself apart with—wars fought with words and arguments debated with bombs, earthquakes in the East and tsunamis in the West, children holding guns instead of books.

This World has heroes. A black orator who has a dream, A single mother with a penchant for Twitter. An anti-apartheid president jailed for twenty and seven years.

They come in all shapes and sizes and they stitch and tape this bleeding world like one would put a Band-Aid on a missing limb and yet they do it anyways and are peerless in their efforts and I admire them.

I tread carefully through This World, because—I might leave an online footprint, I might offend a demographic, I might break the law.

I weave myself through This World and sometimes I come upon a gem.

I find a story so perfect or an insight so profound that This World stops and only starts when I notice it again. I discover a song that nourishes my soul or a poem that just asks to be read aloud with gusto.

But works from the likes of Coupland and Hofstadter are like patches of sunlight in a dense forest and the Don McLeans and Yates of this world are few and far between.

When I find these intangible objects of nonpareil in This World, I take them with me back to My World. They decorate the halls in My World and give me comfort when This World becomes too much to bear.

My World is a library. I've only read through a fragment of its literature.

Some dusty books sit on the shelves of My World, crinkled half-forgotten memories from another age. Some have been read recently. They stand on the shelves and the tables and have creases and folds in them, marking cherished moments and important lessons. The rest have spines that have never been bent and empty pages, and I can only wonder where they will take me.

I have a book open in front of me now. I clutch it with passion and eagerness and my hands as I scribe my life onto its pages.

I give thanks once a year and I enter tryptophan-induced sleep I expect gifts on certain days and I expect to be pampered I favor metallic beasts that run on black gold instead of ambulating when I move and when I move I tend to

always move with a purpose and in This World there isn't ever time for self-reflection no time to pause and take it all in no moment that I can stop and

no place that I belong to no body to hold on to no belief to calm no inner peace

no passion no me

NO.

I am—my self, my beliefs, my own temple, my postulations, I speak my thoughts, I root for the underdog, I vote for the lesser evil, I celebrate the small victories, I depart with a destination in mind, but I also take the time to pause to think, to reflect, to record my recollections into my book, and to archive my book into the library that is my life, and I understand my contemporaries and I relate to my peers, and I know turkey-eating doesn't make me drowsy during Thanksgiving, and I know My World amounts to nothing more than one drop in an endless ocean.

Yet what is any ocean but a multitude of drops?

My Mistake—You don't understand what I'm writing about. (but that's okay)

The idea for this piece came up in response to a personal statement prompt in the University of California applications.

I eventually figured out that this incarnation of my sleep-deprived mind was definitely not meant to be in the hands of an admissions officer at wit's end after a long day of poring over essays. So I took it upon myself to mould and splice my college application essay into something more interesting.

Having recently read a mixture of John Green, Hemingway, and Richard Brautigan, I felt an urge to craft a sentimental and incomprehensible piece that reads like an excerpt from A Farewell to Arms or In Watermelon Sugar.

I tried to throw in an excess of obscure literary devices. Go ahead, tell me if the zeugma I snuck in was actually a syllepsis or vice versa, because I certainly can't tell.

Keep in mind that I am experimenting with my writing. Some of you might not like the sudden shift in syntax, style, or tense, but at least I'm not trying to emulate James Joyce when he wrote Finnegans Wake.

I made a critical distinction between This World and My World. I'm still trying to figure what the distinction is.

The closing line is taken directly from David Mitchell's Cloud Atlas. Any book shortlisted for the Booker Prize deserves to be praised and revered and have its last sentence transplanted.

Since I'm Canadian, it's also my obligation to apologize.

I apologize for forcing you to sit through something that is two pages long.

I apologise for mixing spelling variations in the English language.

I apologize for stealing an amazing line from a good story.
I apologize for not being Ernest Hemingway.
I hope you enjoyed reading this piece.
I hope it makes you think.
Because that's apparently what poems are for.
Without wax,
Kevin Lee

About the Author: Kevin lives in Vancouver, Canada, and is an advocate of universal access to education. He is the president of an international nonprofit and organizes several youth-run organizations. He hopes to pursue a legal degree specializing in information technology tort law.

You can find out more about Kevin here:

http://about.me/uniquelykevin

http://linkedin.com/in/findkevin

High School Attended: St. George's School, Vancouver, British Columbia, Canada

The Process: I interpreted the prompt loosely, and started off with blank verse poetry. I tried embracing an unorthodox college essay to grab the attention of the admissions officer; my essay would be refreshing compared to endless stacks of paragraphs.

When I reviewed my essay with my mentor, he said that it was brilliant—but too risky and abstract. So I did what any good student would do, take the abstraction to the extreme! I played with literary devices, tried to sound like my favorite writers, and for the first time I had fun writing something.

I hope you enjoy reading it. Cheers.

Acknowledgments: Paul Nathan, UC Berkeley Alumni, English 101 Lecture

WHEEL OF GENEROSITY

Austin Lloyd

Was it being adopted that most shaped my identity? Parents wanting another child but unable to conceive one? A woman needing to give away a baby she loves because of her mental illness. Her selfless decision to sacrifice her maternal relationship with that baby (me!) so I could have a more stable life was a parable of love that has informed how I interact with the world. While growing up, we visited her regularly and I observed how dysfunctional her life was and how her decision gave me the opportunity to live a much more harmonious existence.

My adoption is but the prologue. I think chapter one begins with me getting the common cold when I was in the second grade. My dorky upstairs neighbor, Tracy, kindly offered to lend me a story because I was home sick. A second mother to me, she guided me through her home to a bookcase loaded with books on tape. Tracy chose for me the first of many to come. As I examined the covers I could tell they were books of chivalry. I took the book on tape she recommended downstairs and my mom got things set up for me. I got comfy on the couch, and my mom pressed play. I listened absolutely captivated. That was the beginning of years of reading while lying on my bed or outside in the garden.

In the years that followed, those stories had as profound an effect on me as the books of chivalry did on Don Quixote de La Mancha. I developed a worldview founded on the chivalry portrayed in the books, and I became a knight. That is what I have been ever since. What is a knight? To me, it is someone who devotes his/her life to the pursuit of helping others.

Now I am not going to go parading around college campus on my steed saving damsels. I am going do what I can in this real world to make it a better place. In fact, I have already begun. To celebrate diversity, to be assertive, to understand how everything is interconnected, to resolve conflicts, to be empathetic and to believe they can change the world— these are the skills we taught campers at the Mosaic Project's Outdoor School, whose mission it is to "work towards a peaceful future." One night, one of the kids had violent rages, traumatic to the other campers and myself, and was unable to sleep. I stood by his bunk in the pitch black of night rubbing his back slowly, easing him into slumber. I had little rest that week, but never lost my energy or enthusiasm for helping those kids. This experience forced me to leave my comfort zone and find a well of compassion within myself. When the week concluded, my heart expanded into my whole body and out into space from the profound contentment I felt from having planted seeds of peace in the spirits of those children. My hope is that they will rise up and plant their own seeds in the spirits of all those whom they touch.

I now understand that whether it is sacrificing your beloved child, adventuring as a knight or teaching—generosity is supreme. I am eager to see what I can do for and learn from the world in chapter two.

About the Author: I live and grew up in Berkeley, California. After attending an alternative elementary school and getting involved in social justice, I now aspire to get involved in governmental policy related to education. I want to teach in primary schools, I want to teach special education, I want to become a school administrator, and I want to get a doctorate in education research.

High School Attended: Berkeley High School, Berkeley, California

The Process: I began writing my essay around a month before the due date. I went through too many drafts to summarize each one. The length of the essay ranged throughout the process from over two thousand words to only a couple hundred. I had some lines I wrote that just "fit" and others I ended up scratching. I got revision assistance from an excellent college advisor. At times the process resulted in me staring at an empty page for hours, and at other times inspiration struck. I am happy with the final result.

Austin Lloyd will be attending Warren Wilson College.

FORWARD

Chloe Lopez-Lee

I wouldn't know his name if I saw it.

I wanted to etch my father's name on my shoulder, but I cannot read or speak Korean. My mother was hesitant to hear the word "tattoo" escape my lips, but I've always been strong-willed.

So, we struck a deal: On my eighteenth birthday, she will reveal the characters that spell his name, reminding me of the culture he and I shared, and the loss my mom and I shoulder. My decision, to engrave the flowing calligraphy on my skin, will follow.

My dad was in the precinct locker room, dressed in his navy blue uniform, when he collapsed. After he hit the floor, he lost his brain function. Days later, and less than a month before my eighth birthday, he died.

Soon after, my mom gave me his police I.D. card. It was practical, not a sentimental gesture. She wanted me to have it for protection, so that if I encountered officers, I could show I was one of their own.

However, to me, the pliable plastic card with its grainy photo provided a different type of security: a reminder of my dad's eternal wish to keep me safe, and that I was loved, and am loved.

I remember my seven-year-old body thumping between the Sentra's fuzzy seat and its rough seatbelt. I remember the childish excitement of my head pressed against the back of the seat when my dad accelerated.

A week after his funeral, I returned to the smell of crayons and bleach; the comfort of my elementary school. I pushed open the wooden classroom door, and was greeted by the tightest hug I've ever received from thirty-two friends.

Every day after, their support resonated as they whispered, "Go Chloe!" for correct answers in class. They helped me move forward, even when we transitioned to high school.

There, I learned about harmony. I joined Glee Club and, as a junior, became its president. As Glee members sang together, we learned to complement one another; my light, airy soprano would meet the warm tremor of an alto, as each of us melded our voices with the others.

Some days, I hit high notes alone.

For nine years, I studied solo consonance, practicing styles from Italian opera to jazz. These sessions led to performances on a Christmas float parading through Little Italy and at the SoHo Playhouse downtown. I had no voices to accommodate, but also none to cover my mistakes. Yet when my voice squeaked on a high C, I moved onto the next note, refusing to linger on a mistake. I learned to accept my range, and my limits.

After my dad died, I couldn't let his death limit my progress.

I was in the driver's seat now.

In 2012, my uncle succumbed to a fire. He was the sixth man we'd lost. As for my mother, I knew I couldn't control her commute and workload, but I could control what happened at home. Helping her find strength in death was my duty; my dad would've done the same.

So, when she came home I would boil the *pasteles* we'd made a few weeks prior, hoping the taste of *masa* and *carne guisada* would rekindle warm memories. She recounted my first paper cut from the cooking paper, and how I fell asleep with dried banana paste on my cheek. She would remember us making the recipe my grandmother had brought from Puerto Rico and preparing 100 pasteles from scratch for Christmas.

If my father has been watching me from seven to seventeen, I know there are times he'd be shaking his fist down at me, threatening to ground me. But I also know that he'd be proud that I've learned to push my boundaries, make my own decisions, my own mistakes. He taught me the power of moving forward; now I'm ready to learn something new.

About the Author: I am a senior at Eleanor Roosevelt H.S. in NYC, and have lived on the Lower East Side for the past seventeen years. I live with my Puerto-Rican mother and younger brother, who is now twelve years old; my goal is to advance healthcare in areas of poverty.

High School Attended: Eleanor Roosevelt H.S., New York, NY

The Process: Writing my essay was a lengthy process; I drafted it eight times. Even before I literally wrote it, I spent many days freewriting to determine exactly what was essential to my identity. For me, the mesh of hobbies and life events in my essay is a relevant summation of my life (at least in 650 words). Finding what truly matters to me made writing this essay more enjoyable than tedious, and as a result it is one of my favorites.

Acknowledgements: My mom, for reading it even when I had finished my eighth draft.

Chloe Lopez-Lee will be attending Mount Holyoke College.

Some students have a background or story that is so central to their identity that they believe their application would be incomplete without it. If this sounds like you, then please share your story.

SPEAKING FOR LOGAN

Amanda Lowery

Growing up, some said that I spoke just to hear the sound of my own voice. As I transitioned from a talkative tot to an even chattier child, I wasn't afraid to wield my verbal sword. Yet when my brother was born, my twelve-year-old self was stunned into silence . . . temporarily. The moment Logan Lowery set his penetrating gaze on me, for the first time in my life, I found no words adequate to say to him.

Over the next two years, Logan began acting differently than other kids his age. He developed strange habits and twitches, walked on his toes, and most alarmingly, didn't talk. Although his strange behavior made others feel uncomfortable, I loved him unconditionally and even found it endearing that he danced with joy when I played the piano for him.

It was a Wednesday afternoon when Logan was diagnosed with autism. Our loving family environment transformed into a serious atmosphere full of treatment and therapy. My worried parents began to focus their complete attention and efforts on improving my brother's condition, and I soon found my voice and opinion too loud, unhelpful, unwanted. And so I simply stood in silence while my brother's routines . . .

crying when toilets flush, opening doors one, two, three times . . . grew worse.

My parents and I learned to make adjustments, although some were admittedly harder than others. My brother attended numerous therapy sessions weekly, which took a toll on my family's income and well-being. Since paying for a full-time caretaker for Logan was expensive, it was more cost-effective for my mother to quit her full-time job and care for Logan instead. I stopped seeing my parents' faces in the stands at my field hockey games, but I realized that they needed to expend more time and energy on Logan. Although I accepted their priorities, I still admitted that it hurt to be left out.

Finally, one of the therapists suggested that our family try to talk to Logan as often as possible, so he would become familiar with social behavior. I became his most frequent conversationalist, even if the social interactions were still mainly one-sided. One day, in the midst of a tantrum, I flashed my biggest grin and uttered the beautifully written Fox in Socks. Throughout the course of the book, throughout the dips and turns of the tongue-twisters, my brother's mood transformed to pure elation. At his favorite parts of the book, he leapt in the air and flailed his arms. In Logan's case, actions speak louder than words, and I now understand that.

However, sometimes Logan wanted to speak out, but he didn't know how. When he's upset, he starts jumping and shrieking. One day in the grocery store, it simply looked like a temper tantrum. One man exclaimed, "What's the matter with your kid? Doesn't he know some manners?" My mother seemed at a loss for words, shaking in fury and sadness, but in that moment, my calm response was a reflex: "My brother is autistic. It's a neurological disorder, and he can't control his behavior."

That's when I realized that some people don't express their emotions through words. That's when I realized that silence can be the loudest sound. That's when I discovered the power of my own voice. By being second-in-command of Best Buddies, a club for teenagers with mental challenges, I help create awareness about people with special needs in our community. Likewise, my participation in Speech and Debate helps hone my speaking abilities and inform others about social issues. As the vice president of our team, I speak for those who cannot.

Logan's inability to express himself caused me to realize that I needed to utilize my own self expression. In the future, I aspire to be a voice for others by being a mental health advocate. I aspire to speak for Logan.

About the Author: Growing up in sunny Carlsbad, California, I've learned to appreciate my surroundings. I involve myself in an (almost) overwhelming amount of activities—speech and debate, Best Buddies Club, varsity field hockey—and I aspire to become an electrical engineer and special education advocate.

High School Attended: La Costa Canyon High School, Carlsbad, CA

The Process: I was playing piano one afternoon, and I realized that my little brother Logan has never failed to dance whenever the piano is playing. All of a sudden, I found myself abruptly getting off the piano bench to find a pen and paper; I started jotting memorable stories about Logan.

Acknowledgments: Logan, my little brother and big source of inspiration. Dori Middlebrook, my college counselor.

Amanda Lowery will be attending MIT.

MY TWO WORLDS

Noah Lourie

When I first moved to Whitethorn, among the coastal redwoods of southern Humboldt County, I admired the beauty but couldn't escape the feeling of isolation. Whitethorn is a tiny rural place, 200 miles north of San Francisco, and I moved there when I was seven. We live down a narrow, windy, dirt road; besides the post office, the only real public building is a lumberyard. The nearest stoplight is 85 miles in either direction. Being alone in the wilderness, the nearest town 30 minutes away, and a lack of opportunities both academic and non-academic, gave me the feeling of sequestration. The fact that I had lived in the Bay Area all my life, and was therefore cognizant of all the opportunity and community I had left behind, only amplified this feeling.

My elementary school was very small: only 52 students in eight grades and only seven people in my class. Nestled amongst beautiful redwood trees and lush open meadows was our three-room schoolhouse. I worked hard to find friends but there were so few kids and it was hard to fit in. None of the other students had ever lived in a city and most of them rarely left Humboldt County. It made me feel more alone and, instead of friendships, I focused on my school work, my family, and life on our homestead.

Why did we move to Whitethorn? My father had become exhausted with the pace of the Bay Area and wanted a drastic change. I remember while living in Oakland, he would leave our house at six a.m. and often return at eleven at night. I rarely saw him. In Whitethorn, we took our twelve-foot boat down to the ocean to fish. Sometimes it was too rough to navigate and we hurried closer to shore. Other times we would explore the nearby King's Range. We hiked, fished, hunted, and spent time together in nature. Finally, we had time to develop our relationship. Whitethorn gave me an appreciation for experiences I could only have in the country and a chance to spend time with my dad.

As I was about to enter high school, it became clear that Humboldt County could not offer the same educational opportunities that I could get in the Bay Area. The local high school was almost two hours away by school bus and was facing extreme financial challenges. Of the forty graduating students in 2008, only five reported plans to attend a four-year college. As a family, we have always placed education as a high priority, and we decided it was time to return to the Bay Area; I moved back with my mother and sister when I was thirteen. Although my mother and father are still happily married, my father did not come with us. He had found happiness living a more simple life, running his own construction business in Whitethorn. My parents decided that we would commute home every weekend to be together as a family.

Although I had so longed to return, coming back to Berkeley was a complete shock. I felt like I had come back home; at the same time, I had left another home behind. I returned to my old school to finish eighth grade, and I had to fit back in with my childhood friends. I had to figure out how to live in an urban area again. I had to learn how to live without seeing my dad every day.

My years living in Whitethorn were rewarding and difficult—and unforgettable. I learned to appreciate the natural world, to be self-reliant, to work hard. I learned how to spend time by myself and how to be adaptable. I learned the value of opportunities, and the importance of a quality education. Although I left Whitethorn to return to the Bay Area, the lessons I learned there will never leave me.

About the Author: My name is Noah Lourie, I live in Berkeley, California. My goals in life are to become a successful politician, but most importantly to find happiness.

High School Attended: The Athenian School, Danville, California

The Process: For this essay, I began with a complete free write, some punctuation, but no distinct paragraphs or structure. I then read everything over, and moved it into place. After this, I began an edit to cut it down so it fell within the word limit and was grammatically correct.

Noah was accepted at Brandeis University and will attend in the fall of 2015 after a gap year.

ONE

Andy Ly

The majority of teenagers despise their parents nagging, but I was deprived of incessant parental reminders, such as; "Andy, go clean your room!" When I was twelve years old, my parents went through a harsh divorce. My dad relocated to Vietnam, and my mom decided to move to Wyoming. Back then, I longed to have parents who would be available to teach me how to drive or lecture me before my first date, but all that I received were a few checks to make up for them not being in my life. Both started new lives with their new families, and neither of them asked me to go along with them. Instead, my aunt took me into her household. She is the "mother" with whom I still live with to this day.

With all of these drastic changes, it became necessary for me to grow up quickly. Not wanting to be dependent on my guardians, I strove to be self-reliant from the beginning. Part of me was definitely frightened at the pace at which I was obtaining crucial life skills and learning how to provide for myself, such as preparing my own food, but the other part of me wanted to prove to my family, especially my parents, that I was capable of surviving on my own. I wanted to prove to them that I was a son they should have wanted to keep. I wanted them to appreciate me, to be proud that I was their son.

Adapting to the rapid changes in my life, I became my own parent because my aunt and grandmother worked long hours. Growing up, I learned to resolve all sorts of challenges and obstacles rather than asking someone else for help. It took a toll on my youth and shaped my perspective on the future by taking away the innocent and carefree attitude that enable children to be children. I was a twelve-year-old who had to find food before finding my toys.

I appreciate the struggles that I overcame; without them, I would not have become the self-sufficient young man I am. The world of my family—my aunt, grandma, and myself—has prepared me well to attend an institution of higher education. Rather than using my past as an excuse to slack off, I allowed it to feed my ambition to emulate the performance of others who were better off. I have realized that after having few resources and being engaged in technology, I want to create an advanced system that allows other students to have an equal chance to achieve higher education and ultimately their dreams. At the University of California, I want to do in-depth research in science and technology, to develop ideas and methods that will give others an equal opportunity to be successful in life. One particular project that interests me is 3-D printing, which is able to turn digital files into tangible three-dimensional objects. These printers can be placed in areas all around the world that do not have the necessary resources such as tools and supplies for school. This is not meant to replace hard work but to give a boost to those who do not have the same privileges as those who are succeeding in education by allowing them to focus on learning more than working.

Being born in the Millennium Generation, I am aware of the critiques from society about how people born in those years are dependent and egotistical. I believe that I do not live up to this label, and I am determined to continue a life of independence while working towards my philanthropic vision of closing the achievement gap. My lack of resources in the past has inspired me to make sure that all motivated students who want to excel in school have the proper supplies they need to do so.

About the Author: Coming from a Title I school has shaped my goal of giving back to the community. I plan on using an engineering degree to change the way people look towards the world.

High School Attended: The Preuss School, San Diego, California

The Process: In-depth reflection of my entire journey through life was the key to gather ideas to write this essay.

Acknowledgments: My counselor, Ms. Boquiren, and calculus teacher, Dr. Weber.

Everyone belongs to many different communities and/or groups defined by (among other things) shared geography, religion, ethnicity, income, cuisine, interest, race, ideology, or intellectual heritage. Choose one of the communities to which you belong, and describe that community and your place within it.

A LANGUAGE OF ITS OWN

Ian Marzke

Sailing has a language of its own—no stability, no roads, no brakes, no dryness. The only guarantees are rope, metal, ratcheting blocks, and the feel of the tiller in my calloused hands. I speak this language fluently, but to those that are newcomers, it is gibberish. Ever since age three, when I was guided by my parents to steer the family's 24-foot sailboat, I knew I had found my native tongue—I was a member of the sailing community.

Through teaching, I have found my place in this community. Here, it is my job to pass on the language of sailing to others. I scribble wind directions and proper sail trim onto an old, dusty blackboard, students' gazes slowly drifting away—teaching on dry land doesn't do the language justice.

Crawling into a small sailboat with a group of young students, I am in my element. Here, we rely on a set of beaten sails that capture a breeze, flex, vibrate, and force the fiberglass hull through the cresting waves of Lake Michigan. I show the eager students where to sit, how to read the wind, and how to properly hold the tiller. Here, we don't worry about stoplights or traffic jams, just the open water and power of the breeze. Some students are anxious or nervous at first, but after a short time, they begin to comprehend the language. Just as my parents did for me, it's my job in the sailing community to pass on a language thousands of years old.

(The idea of using 'language' as a thematic element came to me after reading the poem called "The Icelandic Language.")

About the Author: I live in the small town of St. Joseph, Michigan, which is in the southwest corner of the state along Lake Michigan. My goals in life include practicing medicine and living a healthy, active life.

High School Attended: St. Joseph High School, St. Joseph, MI

The Process: To write this essay, I took a poem I had written a few months prior and rearranged the content into paragraphs rather than stanzas.

Acknowledgments: Mrs. Klusendorf, English teacher

LEMONADE

John McAndrews

"Why isn't anyone buying my lemonade?" My parents explained to me that it was complicated, "You won't understand until you're older." Challenge accepted. I knew there was a way. I changed my recipe—more sugar, more water, and fewer lemons. Cheaper and better tasting! I made flyers and went door to door handing them out. My little brother was coerced into coming along with a big smile and colorful flags. Little did I know, I had just used math, science, psychology, and art to create a winning formula.

One year later, while wandering the aisles of Costco, I realized candy was in high demand, but parents wouldn't supply it. I emptied the piggy bank, purchasing as many pounds of wholesale candy possible. The candy made its way to my elementary school, pleasing everyone. Classmates got their candy; I magically filled my piggy bank higher. The more money I accumulated, the hungrier I got to discover new strategies. Looking back, I didn't care for the money. It was the challenge; the challenge of multiplying my money was exhilarating.

My childish charm, along with the candy and trading card businesses atrophied, but my curiosity didn't. In 8th grade, I entered the eBay challenge. I understood there was an underlying science to it that was not widely discussed, thus, I explored. I meticulously followed several auctions, fascinated by the seemingly unexplainable discrepancies. eBay was an irrational market; it didn't make sense. Why did identical products sell for vastly different prices? Was it the pictures? The description? Maybe it was the listing time or the title's keywords. After taking notes for weeks and following website traffic, I came to some conclusions. I should use a 7-day auction and list items at 5 p.m. Pacific Time on Sunday night; no other time had more United States traffic. I should use clear pictures with multiple angles and a detailed description that always includes the retail price, box, and accessories in strategically different fonts and colors. I should add a "Buy-it-Now" feature that is intentionally too high but notifies the buyers of the bargain they could get. This leads to buyers who are aware, comfortable, and confident they are buying the right product. If the satisfied customer came first, the seller was successful in the long run. I was ready to start selling.

Of course, eBay was not enough. I wanted to find a way to apply my freshly acquired Algebra 1 and history knowledge. I knew there was more to research than eBay and micro-level businesses, so I dove into the stock market. It was perfect; there was an infinite amount of information available that I could read for hours on end. With the money I had earned, I set up an E-Trade account and dangerously plunged in during a recession. Four years later, my portfolio is outperforming the S&P 500, and I continue to learn more every day.

Unbeknownst to me, it took seventeen years to realize what I had been researching extensively is called "economics." Numerous subjects fascinated me—science, math, technology, psychology, art, and the environment—that all happened to be roughly summed up into one field. Intrigued by this, I threw myself into the study of economics. As economist Greg Mankiw instructs, "think like an economist." I soon realized I had been doing so my whole life, but I sometimes forgot that "there is much more to life than what gets measured in accounts." Economics can answer more important questions than: "Why isn't anyone buying my lemonade," or "how can I fill my piggy bank?" I now ask: "How can we

About the Author: I live in the greater Los Angeles area, and I strive to make the most of what I have and give everything full effort, whether I like it or not. I keep a strong balance between being a social, student-athlete who knows how to work hard and focus while still enjoying life through friends, family, and the outdoors.

High School Attended: Loyola High School, Los Angeles, CA

The Process: Prompt: You may wish to include an additional essay if you feel that the college application forms do not provide sufficient opportunity to convey important information about yourself or your accomplishments. You may write on a topic of your choice.

My school counselor knew I was a really passionate guy who liked to learn and explore but didn't think that was completely visible in my application. He luckily advised me to just tell an honest story that showed I was hungry to learn.

I took his advice and wrote this essay in just one (long) night. It actually was incredibly easy to write, and I made very few changes to my first draft. It was a fun and honest essay that I believed showed an aspect of my life that I was passionate and excited about.

I brought it to my counselor and he was excited because he said it was "so you!"

Acknowledgments: : Counselor and English teacher

TO BABSON AND BEYOND

Nikita Viktorovich Medvedev

I never had an easy time "defining" myself. When I found some definition I thought I liked or could agree with, I'd find a flaw. So when I saw
this prompt, I was automatically at a loss.

I could say I define myself as being a studious and work-minded lad
or as a carefree yet efficient student. I could say that having a job through
the end of junior year helped solidify me or that having two of them
grounded me senior year. I don't have one definition; I am a person of
multiple facets, of multiple likes, dislikes, a person with infinite ideas and
of many niches. Every single day my definition changes, I am not like a
word in the dictionary, I am not set in time but
rather constantly changing, evolving and expanding.

I do have one thing going for me though. Wanting to be a business
major usually means that the student hungers for money or power, holds
on to an idea that Hollywood movies pump out of fast cars and fat bank
accounts. I'm not going to lie, that would be awesome, but the wealth
isn't the only thing I'm looking for in a business degree. Instead, I want
the freedom. I know firsthand how a degree in business can change a life,
how it can open doors no other profession or career can. I was born in a
small city in the middle of Siberia. My mom was also from there. She
had no connection to Moscow or abroad, so when she found a job that
took her to Moscow and then around the world, I realized that she
stumbled upon endless possibilities.

Well, I understand that now, I was like six then, but still.

It's funny actually, that when she found out I wanted to go into business, she was disappointed. She told me of nights without sleep, looking at numbers and plugging away at a calculator. She told me about the deadpan, laborious days she spent at the office at the behest of her boss. But that never scared me, that never put me off. I realize anything good doesn't come easily, that you can't go anywhere without a few sleepless nights. I do not have any delusions of grandeur because I know what it's like to work, I have two jobs at this very moment and the only reason I'm not at one of them right now is a blizzard.

So maybe I define myself as a realist.

About the Author: Name's Nikita Viktorovich Medvedev, I am as Russian as a dacha but live in New York City and want to go into business. Get them fat stacks.

High School Attended: New Explorations into Science, Technology, and Math School, New York, NY

The Process: I sat down, said, "I gotta write this thing." Wrote it.

Acknowledgments: AP English literature teacher, Ms. Palmer.

Nikita Viktorovich Medvedev will be attending SUNY Stonybrook.

LOST PONYVILLE

Apriele Minott

As I was sitting in the back seat while my dad drove us into Randolph for the first time, I saw a sign on a tree. It was not your average lost dog sign, but a sign for a lost pony. That is when my life changed. I had never seen a sign for a lost pony before. People from Plainfield, where I lived before, never had ponies, let alone lost one! Plainfield was a lot more urban. Plainfield had a lot more African Americans. "Lost Ponyville" was going to be interesting.

I did not know how big of a difference Randolph would be until I had my first day of school. All I saw was white. White students, white teachers, white everything. I thought to myself "You're not in Plainfield anymore." I knew that there had to be some blacks here. Our realtor did say there is a 1.6 percent African American population. I assumed that they just blended in with the whites. I was wrong. Walking into the lunch room for the first time was when I realized it. Cross-racial interaction didn't really happen in Randolph. There were tables and tables of white students and then in the corner, there they were, the African Americans. Something felt wrong about this picture. Why didn't blacks and whites interact with each other? I later found the answer.

It happened while Barack Obama was running for his second term of presidency. One night, there was a heated debate between Obama and Mitt Romney. Now being in high school, I didn't think most students would care about the debate. Once again, I was wrong. Following the debate, a student in Randolph posted on Facebook, "I am tired of these stupid niggers trying to control our country." And with that, I learned my answer: African Americans were not truly welcomed in Randolph. I then slowly began to realize the racial prejudice. I thought it was strange that I was only African American to be inducted into the National Honor Society. Something was wrong.

It was not okay for a student to post such a comment on Facebook. I thought to myself, "We are one school, one family. We are in 2013! The racial prejudice needed to end. Us African Americans need to stand up for ourselves." And that is exactly what we did.

We needed to make a change, and so we decided to create the Diversity and Anti-Bullying Assembly. As a member and current president of the Diversity Club, I knew that this was not going to be easy. Why would anyone listen to us, the minorities? But we knew that we had to try. Our principal was not sure this would work so we had to do a trial run for the administration. And, what do you know, they loved it! It was now time for the students. None of us knew what the reaction was going to be. One thousand white students looking at twenty African Americans and Hispanics trying to make a difference. But guess what? The students enjoyed it. One girl was even crying!

After the assembly, the administration came to tell us how incredible we were. That's when I knew that we accomplished something pretty big. We even went to other schools to perform the assembly! That day, you could tell people were changed. I'm not saying Randolph is perfect now, there is still more work to be done, but for right now, people think twice before they act.

When I see or hear racial prejudice now, I can look at it and say, "This needs to change" and know that it can. Who knew that I, an African American from urban Plainfield, could make a difference in "Lost Ponyville"? I knew.

About the Author: My name is Apriele. I live in Randolph, New Jersey, and I am a current senior at Randolph High School. I wrote this essay to show that anyone can make a difference, no matter who you are or where you're from.

High School Attended: Randolph, NJ

The Process: I brainstormed about all the experiences I went through and wanted to choose one that deeply impacted me. I then wrote three drafts and had multiple people read and help me edit it.

Acknowledgments: Rhiannon Shade (college counselor)

Apriele Minot will be attending Cornell University.

Describe a place or environment where you are perfectly content. What do you do or experience there, and why is it meaningful to you? (Common Application)

MY HOME AWAY FROM HOME

Olivia Morello

Imagine a room slightly larger than your average closet; it's warm and has a musky, odd smell; there are cages lined up practically wall to wall, and a symphony of odd sounds meets your ears upon entry. This room is my favorite place at my home away from home: the Staten Island Zoo.

I've been visiting the Staten Island Zoo throughout the course of my whole life. It's small; most visitors only spend a few hours here. For me, the zoo is the perfect size. It's big enough to have an ample reptile collection, several large mammals, and a display of native animals. At the zoo, I'm a junior docent. Essentially, it's a volunteer position that allows me to do nearly everything a zookeeper does. I can usually be seen holding an assortment of odd animals at the zoo, everything from domestic ferrets to pancake tortoises.

In addition to holding animals and teaching people about them, I have the responsibility of cleaning and caring for the animals' habitats. Although most teenagers would dread having to clean, it's one of my favorite parts of my day at the zoo. And though most people dread the smell of animals and zoos, they are some of my favorite smells. The animal rooms are quiet and warm; the animals are always eager to see me. When I enter the seemingly cramped, messy room where we keep the small mammals, I know my day will be great. Despite having to clean cages and change bedding and do laundry and sweep, I smile because I know I'll get to hold a playful ferret or be the first to see a new bunny.

While cleaning the animal rooms, I've had some of my best experiences at the zoo. I held my first snake in the reptile room. I watched an owl fly in the mammal room. I watched a keeper feed newborn groundhogs in the nursery. I spent time working with a baby duck and two baby emus. How many teenagers can say they've had firsthand experience with animals like these? How many teenagers can say they've worked in a field they're so passionate about? Little experiences like these are what make my time at the zoo so special to me. They're what make the zoo my favorite place.

While volunteering at the zoo, I gain valuable insight into what it's like working with animals. I also get to teach children about animals and conservation. These are both topics extremely close to my heart. If I convince even just one nervous child not to be afraid of touching the animal I'm holding, my day can be considered a success. I can directly impact the way a child views our world.

The Staten Island Zoo is the one place I am perfectly content. At the zoo, I do everything I am passionate about. I work with and learn and teach about animals. I gain hands-on experience with exotic animals I could not work with anywhere else. When I volunteer at the zoo, I get a taste of my future. Volunteering has not only allowed me many unique experiences, it has solidified my decision to pursue a career at a zoo. Because I am perfectly content at the zoo, I know I will be perfectly content working as a veterinarian.

About the Author: I'm Olivia Morello from New York. For as long as I can remember, I have aspired to become a veterinarian.

High School Attended: Susan E. Wagner High School, Staten Island, New York

The Process: The moment I looked at the Common Application essay topics, I knew this was the perfect topic. "Describe a place or environment where you are perfectly content. What do you do or experience there, and why is it meaningful to you?" Immediately, my home away from home, the Staten Island Zoo, came into my mind. I combined my favorite memories and a summary of my general activities while volunteering at the zoo to write this essay.

Acknowledgments: Ms. K. Hansalik, my AP English teacher

WANT TO WRITE A NOVEL?

Megan Morris

"Hey, Emily. Want to write a novel this month?" I asked.

Emily has always said that I know the difference between a crazy idea and a bad one, and I'd decided that I had found a prime example of the former. During the summer, on a whim, I had registered for an event affectionately referred to as NaNoWriMo. National Novel Writing Month celebrates amateur and aspiring novelists by challenging them to a crazy month of manic noveling and frenzied plotting with the goal of producing a 50,000-word novel in only the month of November. Having never written anything longer than a four-page short story, naturally I thought that this was a fantastic idea and that I had to try it for myself.

By the time November 30th rolled around that year, I had grown infinitely closer to a girl who is now my best friend. For it is only a true friend who would remind me that I can't become the president with a felony conviction on my record and that prison orange is not my color. However, I had barely more than half of a novel, only 30,000 of the necessary 50,000 words. I was still proud, sure, but understandably disappointed in myself. I'm not a person who is very accustomed to failure. For the vast majority of my academic career, everything I'd ever tried had come fairly easily to me. It was rare that I had to work terribly hard for good grades in my classes. Falling short like this was completely foreign to me, and it irked me on a fundamental level. Now this was a challenge. The next year, we recruited several other friends to our quest. I blatantly refused to stumble again. I made a point to tell everyone that I would have a completed novel at the end of the month leaving me with no choice but to shape up or face utter embarrassment. I was single minded, obsessive even. I planned, plotted, schemed, and color coded until I emerged at the end of the month, novel in hand, my inner editor nowhere to be found, my circulatory system containing more coffee than blood, and my sanity still on vacation somewhere in the south of France.

Writing was the best kind of high I could imagine, especially speed writing like this. Just like a high-intensity diet or exercise fad, this was my literary juice cleanse, if you will. In only a month, I had opened my mind to all the possibilities of my imagination and wiped away all fears of failure or of writing something less than worthy of the bestseller list. Nitpicking was too time consuming; I didn't have the time to agonize over every single word (as I'm doing now), only to get down whatever disjointed syllables I could, and, shockingly, this is what produced the most creative stories with plot twists that even I couldn't have foreseen a mere week before. I even found the month's teachings seeping into other aspect of my life. While I have always been a strong proponent of caution and careful planning, the "leap without looking" attitude that NaNoWriMo preaches has led me to change the way I begin all of my writing projects, to treasure every fleeting moment of this fast-moving life, and to realize that some things are worth taking a risk for.

So this November first, for the second consecutive year, Emily and I found ourselves sitting on desks in one of the English classrooms as we turned to a room of slightly scared-looking underclassmen, introduced ourselves as the co-founders of the Authors United Club and asked them, "Want to write a novel this month?"

About the Author: Megan Morris lives in Williamsville, NY, and is planning to attend SUNY Geneseo to pursue a career in political science.

High School Attended: Williamsville South High School, Williamsville, NY

The Process: Founding my writing club is what I'm most proud of throughout my entire high school career, and I was glad that I found a way to combine that story with the tale of how I met my best friend.

Acknowledgments: My best friend and loyal companion, Emily Shelton.

Some students have a background or story that is so central to their identity that they believe their application would be incomplete without it. If this sounds like you, then please share your story. (Common Application)

THE LAKE

Elena Mosher

The lake that day was like glass. The newly budding trees surrounding the water were reflected perfectly on the surface. The sun was hot, and there was a kind of electricity in the air, as if all the new spring life was humming. We were giddy with the excitement of the approaching summer and content in the company of our tight-knit group.

A Northern Michigan girl born and bred, I dove in right away, feeling the cool water rush over my body. The others slowly made their way in, and we splashed around like little kids, carefree and invincible, until we spotted another beach across the water and agreed to swim over.

"You guys go ahead, I'll stay here," Owen said, "I can't swim."

"Really, you grew up surrounded by Lake Michigan and you can't swim? What kind of Michigander are you?" we joked good-naturedly.

We kicked off, leaving Owen and two others in the shallows. Reaching the other shore, I glanced back and thought I saw a figure waving his arms in the water, but I quickly pushed my instinctive worry away, assuring myself everything was fine. It was not until Kurt's frantic shouts pierced through the trees as we walked around the shore back to the beach that I knew my instincts had been right.

"Guys! GUYS!!!"

Through a break in the trees I caught a glimpse of Kurt in the water. "WE CAN'T FIND OWEN!"

The others did not believe him at first, but I could not ignore my instincts this time. I stumbled over sharp rocks and branches and dove in, propelling myself into water that was suddenly not so glass-like and beautiful.

The rest is a blur. It could have been thirty seconds or five minutes before I found him. He was a white shape suspended at the bottom of the dark water. With a rush of adrenaline I grabbed hold of his limp frame and kicked furiously to the surface.

"Owen! OWEN!" I screamed as I broke surface, gulping for air.

There was a purple hue creeping into his pale cheeks and his eyes were opened wide. At that moment I knew somewhere deep inside that he was gone, but I could not give up on him. With strength I never knew I had, I fought to keep his head above water.

I remember the horrible screech of sirens; I remember screaming and screaming for help; I remember the grotesque angles of his arms as we tugged him onto a raft. After they took him away, I remember scooping up his raspberry-red converse and gray T-shirt with The Accidentals band logo on it. He won't want to lose this stuff, I thought.

Waiting in the hospital I imagined that he would wake up, and I would be able to tell him how I had saved his life. That moment never came.

I would like to be able to say that I realized a higher purpose in Owen's death, but death is just sad, and losing Owen left me shaken and confused. Through the pain I eventually found strength, strength to keep doing what he no longer can. I feel him with me wherever I go—onstage where we spent so much of our time together, at school, in my dreams, and especially when I feel the rush of cool water gliding over my body.

His presence reminds me not to take anything for granted. My world turned upside-down that day, like the reflection of the trees in that deceiving, glassy water. I held the body of my dying friend in my arms and lost my youthful innocence. I carry that experience with me forever now, and with it the determination not to waste a moment of my precious time here. I gave Owen everything I had that day, and now I will give as much to all aspects my life. For Owen.

About the Author: I have lived all my life in rural Northwestern Michigan where much of who I am has been shaped by the nature, agriculture, and water surrounding me. In tenth grade, I transferred from the small school in my town to a much larger high school in nearby Traverse City in order to pursue my passion in music and theater. While still keeping my love for music and the arts alive, I hope to study Spanish and global studies in college and work to help people all over the world.

High School Attended: Traverse City West Senior High School, Traverse City, Michigan

The Process: When I began writing college essays, I knew that I needed to write about my friend Owen and his tragic death because of the huge effect that it had had on my life. I struggled in the beginning stages of writing the essay because I could not figure out how to sum up such tragic event in 650 words or less. My English teacher suggested that I just write without thinking about the prompt or the word limit or anything. What resulted was a raw recollection of my memories and feelings, which not only explained a life-changing event but also helped my healing process.

Acknowledgments: Thank you, Mrs. Kelly Rintala, for your unending support and encouragement.

Elena Mosher will be attending University of Michigan.

THE MERCURY CAFÉ

Taryn Mueller

I'm walking barefoot. Grit, glass, and cigarette butts, the refuse of a seedy city is underfoot, but I don't mind the texture—I like to feel the ground beneath my feet. The air is warm, and an urban-metal-concrete scent tinges its edges.

I've been waiting all summer to discover this place, and tonight, I finally get to meet it.

I'm wearing a dress made of sunflower prints. My legs are unshaven, and I have glittery gold eyelids that say "I'm very beautiful, but I might decide to eat you." Somewhere between a saunter and a stride, I make my way across the parking lot.

Crooked red doors creak open, and I'm inside the Mercury Café. I meander through the room painted with roses and head to the back. On the way, I meet the pianist, John, who is 6'5, 65, and has a fluffy, white Mohawk. He tells me I look like summer and I smile.

The people I love wait for me, beckoning me over to their table. They are all different genders: man, woman, trans*, neutral, agendered, and every one of them queerer than the last. These are my people, social justice and activism, intersectionality and calling out problematic things. They brought me here tonight, knowing it would soon become my home.

There's a vase of blooms on the table, and I sneak a sunflower into my hair.

I empty my bottomless purse. Watercolors, quills, and several sketchbooks tumble out. My people perform angry poetry tonight, and I ink their anger in line and direction, sketching their portraits and profiles. My drinking glass turns into paint water, and it grows darker as I add color to my work, vivid reds and oranges, capturing their fury at being considered "wrong." I get to do what I do best here, and I do not get furtive glances but appreciative grins as I paint the world around me. Here, I get to create, to draw things that matter, to change the world through my art. I am angry along with my people for being told I am "not right," but in this café, I belong. Here, I am never hushed, and though I may be quiet while I'm making art, the outside world will fall silent once my art stares it down.

9 o'clock. The poetry slam begins. Every day, the world tells me and every person in this cafe to shut up and sit down, that we're making too big of a deal out of oppression, that we can't make a difference—and tonight every one of us will scream back so loud that the floor under my bare feet will tremble with power.

Angry, broken, and incorrigibly beautiful, the creative and queer underbelly of so-called "normal society" takes the mic. I wait on tenterhooks. In the next few seconds, the calm before the storm, I look around. One poet listens carefully while crocheting. Another shuts her eyes to take in the sound. They may not be blood, but these people, they are my family: writers, artists, queer people, trans* people, activists, and so much more. The Merc gives each one of us a place.

Tonight, we come home. Binding together to express who we are, shaking our fists and stomping our feet, we yell as loud as we can to the world that would silence us: "WE ARE HERE. WE ARE PEOPLE. OUR EXISTENCE IS NOT WRONG, AND WE WILL NEVER STOP FIGHTING." The Merc is the place I will never be subdued, regardless of my gender, who I am, who I love. Here, I will never be lonely.

Sunday evening at the Mercury Café, tonight's the first time I've been home in all of my seventeen years, and I am at my finest, making art, and shaking up the world.

The poet at the mic takes a breath and begins the poem.

I will never be silenced again.

About the Author: Born and raised in Boulder, Colorado, I aspire to be a visual artist, who, on weekends, smashes oppressive social structures.

High School Attended: Peak to Peak Charter

The Process: I responded to the prompt "Describe a place or environment where you are perfectly content. What do you do or experience there, and why is it meaningful to you?" I originally had another college essay written, but after visiting the Mercury Café for the first time (a popular creative community hub, frequently hosting poetry slams), I knew I had to write about it.

Acknowledgments: I'd like to thank my AP lit teacher, Ms. Kristie Letter, for helping me write this, as well as the entire community in the Mercury Café for inspiring me.

Taryn Mueller will be attending Smith College.

AND SO I TRY

Jonathen Munoz

At the age of eight months old, my younger brother was diagnosed with spinal muscular atrophy type 1. The doctors stamped an expiration date on his forehead and handed him over to my parents. My mother still remembers the doctor looking her directly in the eye and saying, "Take this boy home and love him, because he will not live past the age of two. That's all I can tell you." The problem with SMA type 1 is the simple fact that, just like many other degenerative diseases, there is no cure. There is no time. There is nothing worth trying because, according to the doctors, there is nothing to try—no place to start, no place to look. The hope that helps us all through life drained from the room, shaking the ground around my parents and shattering their lives into small shards of what they once had been.

But sometimes, more often than not, life works in mysterious ways. Sometimes a child with two years to live survives well past that age. And sometimes that child, who was not supposed to have a fully functioning brain, is put in all honors classes. And sometimes, when life as you know it is constantly under the threat of collapsing, you can do nothing but try and hope for the best.

I have watched my brother, burdened with this degenerative and le-thal disease, fade before my eyes. I watch as he grows weaker, and I know that every day spent with him is another day closer to his death. It feels as though every single day could be the last—as though one day, he will just be gone. With feelings like this, my mind and heart grow stronger each and every day. I am an entirely different person than I would have been without my brother in my life. I love easily and forgive more easily because the sad truth is, the truth is sad. Life is far too short, and those we love are taken from us far too early. I make friends and I strive to be as friendly and approachable as I can be, but oftentimes it is difficult when my brother continuously deteriorates in front of me.

And so I try. I try to make memories with everyone, specifically my brother and family. I try to help those who need it, regardless of who they are or where they come from. I try to listen when people need me to, regardless of what they may be talking about. I try and I try so that on the day of my brother's funeral, I have nothing to regret. I try, so on the day that it seems like I have lost everything, it will actually be a new adventure starting. I try, so that in the future I can look back and say, "I was there. I did these things and I met these people and I made these memories. I spent that time with my brother. We laughed. We argued. And, for those moments frozen in time and cemented into my memory, our lives were normal. We were okay. We were just like any other siblings in the world. And, now that all is said and done, I would not go back and change a single thing." I try, because when everything that means anything to you can be lost in just a moment, that's all I can do.

About the Author: I live in the small town of Newton, New Jersey, spending most of my time writing and reading. More than anything, I want to become a successful and influential author.

High School Attended: Kittatinny Regional High School, Newton, NJ

The Process: I am not too concerned with what people may think of me, but one thing I cannot stand is the concept of being forgotten. When writing this essay, I felt no different. Those who work for the admissions office in any college must read copious amounts of essays, leaving many essays to be just another piece of paper in a pile. I decided to go with a topic that is not only unique to me, but a powerful one at that. I did not want to be just another essay for an admissions counselor to read—I wanted to be remembered. Thus, I pulled from my personal experiences and fears and wrote this essay.

Acknowledgments: Special thanks to Carol Fishbone and Mary Houghtaling, who make my writing better in every way, and to my brother, who means the world to me.

Jonathan Munoz will be attending Centenary College of New Jersey.

Some students have a background or story that is so central to their identity that they believe their application would be incomplete without it. If this sounds like you, then please share your story.

THE HEADBAND

Claire Ottmar

It started out simply enough—with a headband.

Standing in front of the mirror in my foyer, I must have readjusted my floral headband one hundred times while waiting for my elementary school bus to arrive. Put in on. Thought I was done. Noticed a single stray hair. Took it off. Smoothed my chestnut locks. Put it back on. But it was never quite good enough. My eyes kept fixating on the barely there frizz or minuscule lumps in my hair—tiny imperfections that other people would never have noticed. But, to me, they stood out like flashing lights, taunting me and demanding my undivided attention.

It started out simply enough—with a headband—but little did I know that was only the beginning of a lifelong battle.

Fast forward to three years later, and then it was a bar of soap.

A bar of soap and dry, red, flaky hands. The harsh soap stung my cracked knuckles, as if a million bees were simultaneously attacking them. But nothing—not even the first-degree burns or the unbearable pain or the bleeding that would eventually ensue—could drown out the nagging voice in the back of my mind that said that I was never clean enough. Deep down, I always knew the painful truth: that I could wash my hands for weeks on end and still not be able to silence that torment-ing voice. But that doesn't mean I still didn't desperately try.

Three more years passed, and then it was a computer.

Multiplication signs, division signs, greater-than signs, percent signs. Exponents, too, and even graphs that I had mastered the art of creating. These characters shone against the white background of the Microsoft Word page. As the clock on the computer approached midnight, I pre-pared myself for the well-intentioned comments that would surely come from my middle school peers the following day—the inevitable, "You type your math homework?!" And I, of course, would reply with the same old, rehearsed response: a simple, "Yeah . . . I guess you could say I'm a bit of a perfectionist." This was easier than explaining that typing my homework was my only option, unless I wanted to spend six hours writing a single assignment. It was easier than telling the truth: that I suffer from obsessive-compulsive disorder.

Then, another three years later, it was a door.

A brown, wooden door, to be exact, furnished with a golden knob that shone in the sunlight. It was a door that I would eventually memo-rize—every dent, every nick, every flaw would become ingrained in my mind—as I would walk through it dozens of times over the next few years. Twice a week, it would lead me into the comfort of my psycholo-gist's office: a safe haven where I could openly express my fears, my ob-sessions, my anxieties. The place where I learned that the world wasn't going to end if I received an A- on a test or if I didn't have absolutely flawless penmanship. The place where I found hope, security, and hap-piness for the first time in a long, long time.

It started out simply enough—with a headband—and, to be honest, it has never quite ended. I sometimes still find myself unnecessarily fixat-ing on grades and seeking unattainable perfection, but I find comfort in the fact that my life is no longer controlled by this disorder and its irra-tional obsessions. I find comfort in how far I have come and excitement in how far I will go.

About the Author: I live in Saint Joseph, Michigan, and I plan on attending Butler University in the fall, where I will major in secondary education. I aspire to become a high school English teacher in the future.

High School Attended: Saint Joseph High School, Saint Joseph, Michigan

The Process: I attended a preparatory class for writing college application essays, which introduced me to many examples of well-written essays and allowed me to begin brainstorming my own ideas. I then progressively wrote--and edited--this essay over the span of four weeks and received feedback from a teacher who works at my high school.

Acknowledgments: I would like to thank my parents and Mrs. Bean Klusendorf for providing me with feedback on this essay.

Claire Ottmar will be attending Butler University.

THE SPICE OF LIFE

Tiffany A. Peart

It was the single moment that eventually formed many of the values that I hold today and that will continue to define me; it was this moment that set my heart on fire. It's not like I planned it though, for the moment came during a typical life activity. I did not think anything of it at the time. I am glad it happened, though—and glad it happened in such a simple, unpretentious way. I just did not expect that making my father's jerk sauce would be so life changing.

I was outside during the summer leading into my senior year in high school, perusing through the colorful vegetation decorating my father's garden: giant green zucchini, pungent onions, plump scallions, fragrant thyme and garlic, ruby red tomatoes, and my all-time favorite, fiery scotch bonnet peppers. As my father prepared his rustic grill—I laugh now because I always wanted him to throw it out and get a new, sleeker model like our neighbors had—for cooking our Jamaican feast, I enthusiastically brought a huge platter of food into my parents' kitchen and began to prepare the meat. The moment I started making my father's family's jerk sauce defined my cooking experience, and, later, me, for it enabled me, if only for a short time, to live in the world of my father.

Living a transient life in Jamaica, my father did not know when he would eat or from where his next meal would come. Hence, my father's cooking became something more than just a fun pastime; it became an act of life or death, a true testimony of survival.

I cook to achieve self-realization. The chopping of the tomato, onion, scotch bonnet, and thyme is where we begin and from there these ingredients are brought together with the coconut milk, sea salt, and my father's secret jerk seasoning—the one ingredient he has yet to share with me! The fusing of the ingredients is like the fusing of my world and my father's, a coming together that transcends time, place, and generational experiences.

Nonetheless, both experiences fuse when he and I are in my East Orange, New Jersey home, cooking our favorite Jamaican meals. Now, every Sunday when I come home from boarding school, my father and I prepare our jerk sauce. Where is the value in this single action of creating a family recipe, you may ask? It is the scotch bonnet that shows me that tenacity can always lead to success; if you can stand the heat of that most intense pepper, you can do anything if given enough time. It is the tomato that reveals to me the sweetness of patience; only time allows the fruit to ripen, and only the ripened fruit is worth eating. It is the garlic, onions, and thyme that shows me the power of human interdependence for it is through human connections that we find ourselves. That these values have become a part of who I am today because of a common, everyday activity shared with my father makes cooking more than just cooking. It is what makes life flavorful.

About the Author: My name is Tiffany Peart and I am from East Orange, New Jersey. I am currently attending Oldfields School, an independent, all-girls boarding school in Sparks Glencoe, Maryland. While at a private, four-year university, I would like to major in political science and later attend law school. My goal is to create a more just world through our US legal system as a civil rights lawyer. I will use my tenacity, commitment and legal training to save the lives particularly of those on the economic and social fringes of US American society

High School Attended: Oldfields School, Sparks Glencoe, Maryland.

The Process: I had a lot of difficulty picking a topic for my essay. When I was presented with the question, "What sets your heart on fire?" I wasn't sure how to approach this inquiry without sounding cliché. I kept trying to find one aspect of my life that would represent me well and reveal my passions outside the classroom; I eventually realized that this particular topic wasn't going to just come to me. After days of pondering, I approached my English teacher and we discussed all of the qualities that really depicted the characteristics that made me unique. We continued to throw around ideas until I mentioned how I enjoyed cooking with my father, a native of Jamaica. Instead of talking about how much I love spearheading student council as student-body president or reading the line up as varsity tennis captain, we decided to elaborate on a little detail that had an impact on my life. From there, I wrote down all of the steps and ingredients that are involved in making my father's jerk sauce. In order for this essay to be effective, my teacher and I knew that there needed to be vivid imagery to bring this essay to life. After a few drafts, the essay was completed, and I realized that sometimes the things that make us look weird or the activities that no one notices are the exact qualities that will make us stand out from fifteen thousand other applicants.

Acknowledgments: I would like to personally thank my advisor and AP English teacher, Monique Neal, for brainstorming and helping me make this essay the best it could possibly be. You inspire me to continue my love for English literature and to one day be as skilled a writer as you.

Tiffany Peart will be attending Spelman College.

OPERA AND ME

Miranda Perez

If it weren't for Gaetano Donizetti, I would never have been born. The romantic music of his opera Lucia di Lammermoor brought my parents together when they sang in the Greater Miami Opera chorus in 1984. Twelve years later I was born. Love of opera, the binding force of my parents union, seems to have entered my biological makeup as a genetic predisposition. It's an innate quality in me, just like my brown hair and hazel eyes. The Sturm und Drang and the joie de vivre of opera permeate the life-blood that runs through my veins. Opera has allowed me to learn so much about life. I now understand that it is important to feel intense emotion and that memories can be accessed in surprising ways.

The complexity of our emotions is something that opera deals with in depth. In the aria "Adieu, Notre Petite Table," from the romantic opera Manon, by Jules Massenet, Manon is forced to leave the man she loves and is overcome with sadness. I understand these feelings surrounding my relationship with my father. He has lived in Miami since I was two. When he would visit New York and I would finally have both of my parents in one place, I experienced ultimate happiness. Walking down the street with his hand in my left and my mom's hand in my right, I felt whole. When he would leave, it felt like I would never see him again. It was so painful that I would try to ignore my emotions. Seeing Manon accept her range of emotions showed me that it was okay, and even healthy, for me to do the same. I prefer to understand this and feel the intense emotion I have become accustomed to, than to go back to a place of avoidance.

Memories, like the ones Manon recalls, can be summoned unexpectedly. The way Manon accessed her own treasured memories was through her "little" table. The brown leather couch where my mom and I sit is my "table." My couch conjures memories of my mom shrieking in horror when Adam Lambert didn't win American Idol or when I was eight years old and sobbed uncontrollably when Stephen Schwartz didn't win the Tony award for Wicked. Even the smaller everyday memories of sitting together talking and laughing, can be found in my little couch. When I move away and our time on the brown couch becomes less frequent, it's these memories that I'll hold on to. The couch that once seemed to be a simple piece of furniture now means so much more to me. I am grateful that I've been fortunate enough to realize that.

As a child, while my friends were having sleepovers, swooning over the Jonas Brothers and Hannah Montana, I was going to the opera. When people hear that I love opera they often say, "Wow! You must be an old soul!!" But opera isn't only for senior citizens or the elite. In fact, the stories and the characters of opera are relatable to all of us. Opera plots include revenge, gossip, love triangles, and deception, all aspects of modern society. I find myself completely enthralled by the elaborate story lines, watching opera the same way I watch Pretty Little Liars.

Opera is like a book passed down from my parents that I have read and reread. Its origin is what makes it meaningful and the way it enriches my life is why I hold on to it so tightly. Chapter by chapter, I find a greater understanding of the world and myself. Thanks, Gaetano.

About the Author: My name is Miranda Perez, and I am a New Yorker, born and bred. Growing up in such a vibrant city, I have been surrounded by the arts my entire life. My ultimate goal is to become the general director of an opera company because I know that I would be nothing without opera and need to find a career where it can be a part of my everyday life, without me having to be a performer.

High School Attended: Eleanor Roosevelt High School in New York, NY

The Process: Finally finishing my essay and being happy with it was quite a grueling to process. It was difficult for me to clearly articulate everything that I wanted to say about the topic I chose. After writing many, many drafts of my essay, I reached a point where I felt comfortable with the message I conveyed about who I am and how I see the world.

Acknowledgments: I would like to thank my mother, father, and vice principal for helping me end up with an essay that I was proud of. I couldn't have done it without them.

Miranda Perez will be attending Tufts University.

TIARA TALES AND OTHER STORIES IN THE ART OF RISK TAKING

Chloe Pinkney

All eyes were on me.

I didn't think much of it at first. I figured this was part of being a newbie at sleep-away camp—awkward glances and stares from the older kids who had spent every summer of their childhoods at Shire Village.

It wasn't until I looked in the bathroom mirror in my bunk that I realized I had been wearing a sparkly tiara on my head. The plastic bejeweled crown had been a gift from my grandmother Gwennie.

Looking back, it made perfect sense that I would walk onto the muddy grounds of camp wearing Gwennie's tiara. In our family, Gwennie has always been the one to dive headfirst into new experiences, which she continues to do with flashy style. (To this day, you can spot my grandmother from a mile away with her sequined-and-rhinestone outfits.)

Gwennie was the first woman in my family to go to college. As an African American student in the 1950s, she crossed a line with pride that wasn't visible to the human eye. She stepped past a barrier while wearing her own crown of self-confidence.

It was Gwennie's headfirst fearlessness that had inspired me to wear my tiara on the first day of camp. I had tried the tiara on as a joke at home and loved it so much that I kept it on for the entire car ride.

Then I realized something else. Even though I was embarrassed, I loved my tiara and was not going to take it off. I was surrounded by pine cones, mosquitoes, and dirt, but that wasn't going to stop me from wearing what I wanted.

My sense of style has been that way ever since. Gwennie's glittery tiara inspired my desire to jump headfirst into adventure and to take risks.

In middle school I turned Dad's neckties into funky headbands. In sixth grade my parents let me crop my hair into a short Afro that I later dyed blond. Then I swapped my Skechers for tap shoes and showed everyone that taking risks means walking with my own rhythm.

There have been countless times I've heard people say, "Why are you wearing that?" But that never held me back.

Jumping headfirst has let me say yes when others have said it couldn't (or shouldn't) be done.

Who says an African American girl can't play the grandmother in her school production of Fiddler on the Roof? Taking that risk let me bring my creative determination to the play's dream sequence by performing a solo filled with Hebrew lyrics.

My grandmother's example has shown me that taking risks is never easy. But not taking risks is even harder.

Through my fashion fearlessness, I've learned that real style is about seeing beyond the surface and digging deeper into the true meaning of things.

I've also discovered that the art of risk taking means staying true to my tap shoes and my tiara.

About the Author: My name is Chloe Pinkney. I was born in Spanish Harlem and raised in Brooklyn, where I currently live. I'm a creative thinker with many overlapping passions. In my current role as president of student council, I've enjoyed working with my fellow students and my teachers to help shape my school community. I've excelled in honors English, cross-cultural study, visual communications, public speaking, the mentoring of special-needs students, and hands-on internship work in the fashion and magazine industries. As someone who has many interests, I also have many life-goals. I'd like to become a creative director, stylist, or editor at a national magazine. But implicit in these goals are my larger aspirations, which are to use my creativity to build a global community of creative thinkers and to thus foster tolerance and connection among people.

High School Attended: Churchill School and Center, New York, NY

The Process: Writing my essay was like searching for an obscure jewel that was buried deep inside me. I wanted the essay to show readers the essence of my creative self-expression. To help me "find" the essay, my college guidance counselor held the flashlight while I did the digging! Finally, I struck the roots of my very own family tree, most notably, my grandmother Gwennie, the first woman in our family to go to college and one of the rare African American women in her small upstate, New York town to become a college graduate. The essay I wrote is my personal statement and is also a tribute to my grandmother's bold style and courage that became the inspiration for my essay and have also served to inspire me as a young black woman.

Acknowledgments: My college guidance counselor, Erin Hugger

Chloe Pinkney will be attending Skidmore College. She got in Early Decision.

Describe a place or environment where you are perfectly content. What do you do or experience there, and why is it meaningful to you? (Common Application)

ACTING WITHIN THE
HUMAN KALEIDOSCOPE

Thomas Poston

The stage is my own ethereal realm.

I'm sovereign over it; I control what happens on it, yet I invariably yield to its influence when I enter its domain. "All the world's a stage," but the stage itself contains every world humanly imaginable.

The light on stage is rich amber; blue-white and flushed red often interpose. Heavy curtains shroud the stage in shadow conducive to theatrical magic, but the stage lights, with their low fervor, overpower darkness. Pervasive warmth blends the crisp scents of fresh dust, old books, and dry sweat into one very human sensation, and I savor the familiarity of lingering memories that duet with my tongue, harmonize with the raw stage fragrance, and pirouette around my brain.

I can easily evoke these distinct sensations because I've tightly associated them with theater, a perpetual source of personal fascination. The exploration and exposition of naked humanity that takes place on the stage reveals to me new truth and allows me to communicate powerful emotion to the audience. The stage vividly illustrates every facet, every whispered nuance, of the human experience; it charges naked humanity with a visible, palpable vitality. Viewing a theatrical performance from the audience allows one to experience a fraction of that vitality, but stepping onto the stage and acting in a theatrical production exposes one to the unabridged and unadulterated energy of all theater has to offer. I thrive on that energy.

The embrace of the stage fills me with contentment and overwhelms me with a craving for improvement. As an actor, I constantly pursue the perfection of imperfection. I venture to authentically depict the triumphs and failures of mortal man and to paint portraits of purely human truths. Playwrights dig through the accumulated literary and historical clutter of thousands of years of human existence to choose the key elements of humanity that they wish to illustrate. When I step onto the stage, I'm an independent operative of the playwright, an interpreter of his intricate, meaningful message.

The theatrical mission to communicate the human experience may seem quixotic. Of course, it is impossible for a stage production to accurately and wholly depict humanity, yet I have found no other medium that has rivaled the accomplishment of the tangible, atmospheric, immediate stage. And so I find sanctuary on the stage, portraying a character that has been invented or adapted for some dramatic purpose.

Am I insecure in my own identity? Absolutely not. Theater is humanity's mirror, and my own. I use the stage to understand and refine my identity, not to suppress it. Intimately exploring the qualities of many characters over the years and examining their thoughts, actions, and motivations has allowed me to explore the manifestation of those qualities in me. I've contemplated eternity by portraying a dead soul in Our Town. I've explored the nature of family and the American experience in I Remember Mama. Currently, I'm facing the transformation of a psyche under terrible conditions in The Desperate Hours. Through it all, I've considered these human truths and searched for their presence in me. The stage has become a place of self-reflection and emotional translation; it is my personal meditation grounds, devoted to the study of the human and myself. The energies of my fellow actors, the set, the audience, and the stage itself intensify my personal experience as an actor. Acting is a beautiful test run of humanity, and actors like me are humans who've decided to investigate on the stage a more diverse selection of occurrences and personalities than one individual could ever experience anywhere else.

Being on stage drags open my curtains, cuts on the spotlight, and slams my nostrils with the raw scent of my own humanity; my character and I are poles apart, yet we are the same, intoxicated by the glow of the lights on the stage and enamored with the possibilities we see in the human kaleidoscope.

About the Author: My name is Thomas Poston. I was born in Raleigh, North Carolina, and I'm proud to call the Outer Banks of North Carolina home today. I am a student, an actor, and a dreamer; I aspire to positively influence the people and places that surround me throughout my life by always striving to gain a greater understanding of myself and the world in which I live.

High School Attended: Currituck County High School, Barco, North Carolina.

Process: I wrote the rough draft for this essay after a long night of rehearsal in the theatre. I had extensively contemplated the prompt, trying to think of that one place in all the world where I felt happy, free, and genuine. The stage struck me as that perfect environment. While the essay needed a lot of fine tuning after that initial writing period, the central ideas had taken root. I revised the essay considerably, trying to make it as personal as possible, while also staying concise. Several drafts later, having incorporated some of the suggestions of my brilliant English teacher, I had a finished essay - an essay that carried my voice and reflected my passions in an exciting way.

Acknowledgments: Jon & Anita Poston (my parents); Ms. Valerie Person (my AP Literature and Composition teacher)

Thomas Poston will be attending Wake Forest University.

Some students have a background or story that is so central to their identity that they believe their application would be incomplete without it. If this sounds like you, then please share your story. (Common Application)

EMPOWERMENT

Colette Prideaux

All I knew were my tears. They blurred my vision, tickled my face, and filled my mouth with a salty taste when I tried so desperately to wipe them away. Crying was my only defense mechanism back in my elementary school, and though I was put in the same situation quite frequently, I could never muster enough courage to allow myself to do anything else. So I let the tears flow.

I went to the same school for ten years. Though there were some new additions throughout the years, I was basically stuck with the same class. Academically speaking, I was the same person I am now. I was diligent, studious, and loved learning. This thirst for knowledge was a seed that could have been watered into a beautiful flower, but the process wilted before there was ever a chance.

I was bullied throughout my run at my parochial school. I lived through girls blatantly speaking about me during class, and books being passed around that held endless pages of lies about me. I wasn't even safe at home, because in logging into my email accounts I would find myriads of emails filled with name calling and poisonous verbal abuse. I was battered from every corner. I became the epitome of the generic outcast from middle school movies, the ones that sit alone at lunch. I tried once to alert my principal to some of the actions against me, but she refused to listen. Suddenly, in my bruised middle school mind, it felt like the whole world had this vendetta against me, a malicious mutiny. I was too sensitive, too kind, to fight back. They were all so strong. A lone soldier could never fight against an army that outnumbered her. So I cried.

However, I learned to take the pain I endured and used it for mental enrichment. I challenged myself to rise above their vile actions. My hard work paid off and I was accepted into a prestigious high school, as well as named valedictorian of my eighth grade class. I finished my career there and restarted— something I had been yearning for all my life. Though sometimes I reflect back on these times and feel a surge of hurt, I am thankful for the experiences, as they have given me a true purpose in life. It is imperative that I help young people who are bullied because they need to understand that they are significant, and that their bullies are mere obstacles that they must tackle in order to recognize their self-worth. I want to dedicate my life to this cause, because the issue is getting stronger every day, and I can't stand back and watch kids endure such terrors—terrors that I am all too familiar with.

I made a vow to myself that I would never allow anyone to abuse me again in that way. I realized that I granted all those girls easy access into my inner workings by not standing up for myself. Those tears would be no more, and I would find a new outlet for emotional expression. This is the maxim that my new foundation is built on. Like the prisoners in Plato's "Allegory of the Cave," I rose from the dark and embraced the light. I narrowly freed myself of those demeaning fetters, and if I ever need to escape again I will emerge back onto the battlefield a stronger girl. Ten years of pain have only instilled a drive in me, a will to succeed. While I am not completely secure, I am so much more than that solitary solider.

I am empowered.

About the Author: My name is Colette Prideaux, and I am a senior at Staten Island Technical High School. Though I'm not dead-set on a career yet (my major of choice right now is psychology), in life I hope to help those with disabilities and mental issues.

High School Attended: Staten Island Technical High School, Staten Island, New York

The Process: I devoted most of my college essay-writing time to my common application essay since most of the colleges I am applying to must read it. I knew my bullying story was one I wanted to share because I think it's important to let people know you have a past that has shaped you. If I weren't bullied, I wouldn't be the person I am today.

Acknowledgments: My parents & sister—the most loving and supportive family I could have ever been blessed with

SPICES IN MY ANNIE'S PASTA

Marie-Isabella Rogers

While my parents often work five hundred miles away from our home, my brother, Nathan, and I spent much of our childhood under the care of a series of fifteen belly-dancing babysitters. Their frequent concerns included misinterpreted chakras, candlelit meditations, and adding exotic spices to my beloved Annie's Pasta. My childhood could have not contradicted my parents' Jane Austen-inspired vision of reality more severely. I became increasingly hungry to hear more of my mother's wisdom instead of the mindful mantras of my eccentric babysitters; yet the more I resented their outlandish ideas, the more I was affected by their knowledge.

While my brother mindlessly devoured the egregious pasta, I resisted. Secretly, I felt it was my nine-year-old duty to preserve my family traditions. According to my mother, in a typical Irish Catholic family, at least with New York City roots, the closest equivalent to the Bible is The New Yorker. Our drives were flooded with NPR interviews, classical symphonies, and lectures on Ansel Adams from my father. My parents wanted me to understand the importance of books, culture and art. Most human beings of the teen species make it their mission to distance themselves from their parents, but I was eager to delve into their world of refined tastes.

At first, I was only interested in my parents' perspective, not anyone else's, no matter how insightful. My caretakers, such as they were, were people of a different hue, living their lives fluidly, like roaming gypsies. Disowned by their families, they were searching for acceptance for their

Eastern spiritual interests. Paradoxically, my Jane Austen-esque family was the one that accepted them. Out of respect (and cautious intrigue) modeled by my parents, I made raw kale smoothies with Darje, chose my spirit animal with Elizabeth, and sheepishly danced to Natalie's sitar music. These belly-dancing, nonconformist beings were the unlikely source of an alternative culture that was in stark contrast with my family, and yet, I have collected these individuals in my mind over the years in remembrance of true acceptance and compassion. They were each seeking new ways to exercise their identities, and so was I.

My parents taught me how to interpret and appreciate art, while my babysitters taught me how to feel and be open towards to the unexpected, even in myself. Through artists like Kathryn Bigelow and Jackson Pollock, but also Shadi Ghadirian and Tame Impala, I have come to realize that art is the key with which I open the door to new ideas of expression and emotion. In my pursuit to be an art critic and writer for none other than The New Yorker, I have been given the chance to cultivate my own taste of the world through artists. I am the creator, the translator, and the curator of my own life. No longer a child, I have gradually come to see the world through a lens that is broader and more flexible than Jane Austen in a sari.

About the Author: Marie-Isabella Rogers lives in Oakland, CA, where she attends Holy Names High School. In the future, Marie-Isabella would like to be an art critic and essayist for *The New Yorker.*

High School Attended: Holy Names High School, Oakland CA

The Process: I began my process with a series of free-writes. Then, once I had a clearer sense of what I wanted to write, I wrote several, more formal drafts, until the essay fit the appropriate word count.

Acknowledgments: Thank you to Jessica Brenner; Gabrielle Glancy; my English teacher, Ms. Tussey; and my mother, Marguerite Enright for your help and support.

Marie-Isabella Rogers is attending Sarah Lawrence College.

THE FLYING EFFECT

Marie-Isabella Rogers

It was all about the prestige. I was convinced that rowing would make me a mysteriously cool, preppy kid. Plus, I wanted to be unique and, besides signing up for underwater basket weaving, rowing seemed to be the surest guarantee. I instantly claimed rowing as my "thing": my one talent that embodied the entirety of my identity. Why? It would be a long time before I realized what compelled me.

Maybe it was a lapse of judgment, or better yet, a lapse of sanity. As I quickly found, rowing is physical suicide, a social-life murderer, and a self-esteem breaker: a true test of character. But no one, not even I, would have predicted the worst: I was repeatedly plopped in the F-Boat—the boat of misfits.

Instinctively, I wanted to abandon my rowing dreams, but I would not be a quitter! And so, I rowed on. As the months progressed, I managed to earn recognition as the best in the F-boat: the High Dowager, as I called myself. Yet, even as I improved, I was routinely sling-shotted back into the F-boat. Was I ever going to be good enough to succeed in rowing? I hated myself and loved the sport—rowing allows no lucidity.

Amidst the chaotic reality of rowing, I found myself teaching the confounded sport to Lucy, a girl with cerebral palsy. At first, I cautiously helped the disabled rowers, or adaptive rowers as they are known, trying not to show my apparent curiosity regarding how people could row without essential limbs. But Lucy snatched my arm and jerked me towards an erg.

"Teach me how to row," she instructed. Without hesitation, I did. That day, she erged a 6k, a preposterous attempt even for an able-bodied person; yet she smiled, sweating and panting just as profusely as I did next to her. I had never witnessed someone loving erging so much in my life.

Although it did not occur to me immediately, I know now that it was Lucy who reminded me why I love rowing: the simplicity of rhythm, structure, and composure, gliding on a bliss-wave of unbearable addiction. It is this visceral feeling of peaceful exhilaration that I call the flying effect: the sensation a rower works endlessly towards, but rarely experiences. I saw in Lucy the happiness and accomplishment I felt when I began to row, unaware of any ranking, potential, or quota of success I dared to reach.

Sometimes I wonder why I still row; there is no distinction or honor in it for me. But, Lucy, of all people, propelled me into a greater dimension of understanding. Rowing was never about my appearing the best—instead, it was about finding something that I love unconditionally. Now, though rowing backwards for longer than I am willing to admit, I am able to see clearly, looking forward towards my next accomplishment, when I will set my boat, and row.

About the Author: Marie-Isabella Rogers lives in Oakland, CA, where she attends Holy Names High School. In the future, Marie-Isabella would like to be an art critic and essayist for The New Yorker.

High School Attended: Holy Names High School, Oakland, CA

The Process: Prompt: I began my process with a series of free-writes. Once I had a clearer sense of what I wanted to write, I wrote several more formal drafts, until the essay fit the appropriate word count.

Acknowledgments: Thank you to Jessica Brenner; Gabrielle Glancy; my English teacher, Ms. Tussey; and my mother, Marguerite Enright, for your help and support.

THE HOME OF MY GREAT
GREAT GRANDFATHER

J. Alexander Rumsa

As my grandma and I trekked through the meadow, tall grasses sliced my calves. In this part of the Lithuanian countryside, no power lines crackle overhead, and only a few roads litter the land. The rest of the ground is engulfed by wild weeds and bushes. With my legs streaked with fresh cuts, I asked my grandma, "Are we nearing great great grandpa's house yet?"

"Yes, it should be close."

After tripping through more tangled thorns and acquiring more scrapes, my grandma stopped and said, "We're here." Excited, I swiveled my head right and left scanning for the house—nothing but plants. "Grandma, are you sure this is the place? There's nothing but wildlife here." She then pointed down, and I saw it. A large slab of concrete sat overgrown with flowers and vines. With wide eyes and an open mouth, I stood frozen expecting a house, not the remains of one.

I've made it through a mile of sharp grasses to my family's past home. Shouldn't this be exciting? It's just a concrete base though—nothing too special. But this is where my family used to live. Still unsure of what to think, I sat down on one of the concrete edges to rest my legs. After a few minutes, the rough structure intrigued me and I began to run my hand over the cool stone. Spiders and ants darted in and out of crevices to avoid my fingers. As my hand continued, I noticed a strip of slab turn to a darker grey. Wondering what might have caused this discoloration, I followed this six inch wide strip until it converged with another strip of the same color, and then that one made a 90 degree angle with another strip. That line turned into another 90 degree turn, then ran around the edges of the foundation to make a large square.

Once all the strips were traced I thought, these lines must be where the walls would have stood. Feeling like an archeologist piecing together an ancient relic, I began imagining what rooms went where in the house based on the marks left by the walls.

Walking over to the west side, I began to reason. This part must have been the living room since it has the best view. And the room next to it might have been the dining room. The kitchen was probably in the back corner, and the bedrooms must then back up to the living room.

Reaching into her satchel, my grandma said, "Alex, I found a picture of the house in my bag. Come take a look." Fascinated, my eyes devoured the picture. Two windows faced out on either side of the front door. Seeing a couch through the right window, I now knew my living room prediction was right. Satisfied, I ran back to the concrete, and squatted down pretending I was sitting on the couch. Once settled, I pictured a bulky armchair nestled in the corner and a sizzling fireplace on the far wall. Knowing that I was in the exact place the couch used to be, I peered out where the front window used to stand. I wonder what my great great grandpa saw when he looked out this window 100 years ago? Maybe he looked numerous rows of potatoes and cucumbers. Or maybe there was a neatly cut yard of grass. Well it's too bad there's just a tangled mess of thorns now. But who knows, maybe in the next 100 years my great great grandkids will come back to restore this land.

Knocking me out of my thoughtful trance, my grandma tapped me on the shoulder and said she was heading back. With a new meaning on my great great grandfather's home, I turned and started hiking back to the car.

This may be a crumbling slab of concrete, but this foundation is the foundation of our family.

About the Author: I live in St. Joseph, Michigan, and will be attending DePaul University in the fall of 2014. I plan to study 3-D modeling and animation.

The Process: The idea for this essay sparked when I was traveling in Lithuania with my family. I spent half the summer and early fall writing this piece. After coming up with my first draft, I had friends and family look at it. From their criticism, I reworked the paper and came up with new drafts. I then edited two series of drafts before I had my English teacher overlook them. From her insight, I changed some parts to make more sense and flow smoother. I then fixed some minor errors and then looked it over. Pleased with the results, I submitted it to DePaul.

Acknowledgments: Eileen Klusendorf, Michelle Rumsa

J. Alexander Rumsa will be attending DePaul University.

BACKYARD BIBLE STUDY

Alexander Shultz

When the waves stopped, when the boys' voices quieted down, right at the point at which I no longer felt anxious that I would be seen with them, they started the chaos all over again. They screamed and splashed and hit and waved pool noodles everywhere as I sat on the side and wondered to myself, "Is this really how I'm spending my weekend?" I was participating in "Backyard Bible Study," one of many weekly pool parties sponsored by my church youth group. Not long ago, I was the one in the pool engaged in the pseudo-fights and trying to dunk the other guy, exhilarated. But as a high schooler, I felt nothing but embarrassment while I witnessed the rampant immaturity on display. Later, while I was packing my towel and planning my escape, our youth pastor, Sarah Allen, stopped to talk with me. Sarah had known me since I was the child in the pool, and she'd seen me grow into the conscientious teen that was then desperate to leave. That night she offered me the position of Youth Elder.

Despite the oxymoronic title, being a Youth Elder was apparently serious business. Like other Elders ordained in the church, I would be a part of Session, the governing body of the congregation, and the chair of the Youth Ministry Team (YMT). I remember feeling excited, perhaps due to the naïve notion of power and respect that I would gain with such an important position in the church. I accepted the offer and couldn't help but notice the approval and pride in Sarah's eyes.

Months later, after I had been officially ordained as an Elder, I attended my first Session meeting. On a Tuesday night fifteen people over age 50, a couple of people in their 30s, and I shuffled into a stuffy room bathed in fluorescent light and filled with folding chairs and tables. Discussion began on topics listed in the official agenda, and dry, stark voices motioned and voted on every tedious topic in running a church, while I sat, feeling every point where my clothes touched my skin. I savored the moments where someone would make a joke and people would laugh, but what I wanted more was a problem where I could say something. When the topic of conversation is dominated by Sunday school classes for middle-aged couples or the inner workings of a budget, there's only so much a seventeen-year-old can contribute. I ended up watching the sun set through the west window of the conference room, silent.

The initial dread of Session meetings had tainted my opinion of my position, so it was no surprise when I started dreading my first YMT meeting too. But the discussion at YMT was not about the entire church. It was about the First Presbyterian Church youth group, something I happened to be a self-made expert on. After six years of mission trips and retreats, I was more than ready to lead discussion and planning on YMT. I remember that first time we planned events designed specifically to make incoming 6th graders feel welcome in the youth group that coming summer. In that excitement, in that dialogue where I purposely planned, directed, and recorded discussion, I became aware of the engineering behind those ridiculous pool parties. They were supposed to be loud, and stupid, and have nothing in the way of shame because the most important people were the kids who needed to feel included. Years ago, the people on the YMT had indirectly made me belong, made me feel like people wanted to have fun with me at a time when it seemed like no one at school could stand me. And now I had the opportunity, the privilege to provide a space for inclusion and friendship to the annoying, awkward, and endearing children in which I couldn't help but see myself.

About the Author: I live in Austin, Texas and I want to tell stories through film for the rest of my life.

High School Attended: Liberal Arts & Science Academy High School, Austin, Texas

The Process: The prompt for this essay was to describe an event that marked a transition from childhood to adulthood. I initially thought it was a perfect venue to showcase the responsibility and power I carried as an ordained Elder in the church, but as I went through more and more drafts, I realized the importance of the position was about giving back to an inclusive community that I benefitted from. Ironically, it ended up not being about God or power at all, but simple human kindness and understanding.

Acknowledgments: I'd like to thank Sarah Allen for offering me the position and my English teacher, Mo Harry, for help revising the essay.

Alexander Shultz will be attending Rice University.

LUGUBRIOUS

Bailey Soderberg

If I had to choose a favorite word, I believe it would be lugubrious. First of all, the word just rolls off the tongue. The lavish quality of the enunciation as one vocalizes the word is simply glorious. The first two syllables, pronounced "loo-goo," already have me in hysterics with the foolish sounds that resemble the coos of an infant. Just when I think that the word has reached a climax, the first two syllables are followed up with a very professional and commanding "-brious." Merely murmuring the last two syllables of lugubrious suggests a higher quality of speaking. This juxtaposition in itself is enough to catapult this word to the top of my list of favorites.

Consequently, the nature of this word provides another intriguing contrast. The meaning of the word is defined as "mournful, dismal, or gloomy; especially in an exaggerated, insincere or even ludicrous manner." It is between the somber meaning of the word and the "ludicrous" way that it can be used that has me fascinated. How can one even fathom the ability to overemphasize gloominess to the point of comedic effect? If one has ever been truly somber, they would realize that being in such a state is no laughing matter. I suppose this reflects the inclination of humanity to create comedy out of grief in order to make sense of the world, but it seems too complex of an action for me to attempt. I suppose I can continue to admire the word from a distance, and keep my own lugubriousness to a healthy minimum.

About the Author: My name is Bailey Soderberg, I live in Yarmouth Port, Massachusetts, and I attend Sturgis Charter Public School West where I am part of the International Baccalaureate Curriculum. I plan on becoming an editor or a lawyer; either way I want to major in English for my first four years of college.

High School Attended: Sturgis Charter Public School West, Hyannis, Massachusetts

The Process: The prompt is "What's your favorite word and why?" I was trying to let my whimsical and creative side shine through in this essay to counteract the more strict and serious prompts that most colleges require. As a result, I let my mind wander during the process.

Some students have a background or story that is so central to their identity that they believe their application would be incomplete without it. If this sounds like you, then please share your story. (Common Application)

GRANADA: MY HOME AWAY FROM HOME

Jordon Solomon

"No se cierra Yordan. La ventana no se cierra" Lucrecia said. ("It doesn't close, Jordan. The window doesn't close.") Just an hour earlier I had been jamming to "Got Money" while enjoying a turkey sandwich and potato chips on my flight from Miami to Managua. I now found myself in the passenger seat of a rickety red pickup truck weaving around horse carriages, cow herders, and cyclists riding garage sale bikes. This marked my transition to a new world. I did what I could to block out the rainwater, smells of burning trash and animal waste. Forty minutes later we arrived at my host family's house in Granada, Nicaragua (three bedrooms, one flush toilet, and one sink for eight people). My host mother, Lucrecia, and I were the only two who had stayed dry as the rest of the family rode in the flooded truck bed. Once "home," I entered the living room, and the memories began to come back.

Over two years ago, my friend Noah proposed that we travel to Nicaragua together on a Spanish immersion trip. "Great" I thought, "a way to help people and improve my Spanish!" A week before our scheduled departure, Noah became gravely ill and could not travel. Without his company, I began to regret my decision. When I met my host family, the Davilas, and discovered our common love of baseball, I began to relax. After living with them for one day, I was known as "el tomate" (the tomato), because of my red cheeks.

The most important relationship I developed on this trip was with my host father, Bayardo. Known as the Derek Jeter of Nicaragua, he holds many Nicaraguan professional baseball league records, and remains a national icon. He currently works for the Granada mayor's office promoting youth sports. He is challenged by the lack of equipment in such an underprivileged country.

Bayardo told me the story of one boy who rows across a lake with his father just to get to Little League practice. I would see kids playing ball in the street with a fallen tree branch as a bat, and rolled-up socks as a ball. I thought of all of my old bats and gloves sitting in the garage at home. How could these kids have so little while I have so much? When I traveled home I promised to help fight this inequality and began organizing baseball equipment donations in the Bay Area.

A few equipment collections later I found myself waiting in the airport baggage check line hoisting two fifty-pound duffel bags filled with catching gear, bats, hats, and gloves. Although I had already shipped several bags of equipment to Bayardo remotely, I was now headed back to where it all began.

It was not only what I did for the kids of Nicaragua that made my work meaningful but also the relationships I made and how much I learned from the people that I came to love. When I traveled back to Granada this summer, I grew much closer with the Davilas' adopted son, Rodrigo. It saddened me to see how poorly educated he is compared to me. One day, when I told him that there are millions more people in the US than in Nicaragua, he refused to believe me! Granada is all he has ever known and all that he ever will know.

Although Nicaraguans may have less than us Americans economically, they have more than us in many other aspects of their lives. Grandparents play a bigger role in raising children, people are much friendlier on the streets, and close friends become more like family. Throughout my time in Granada, I became a member of this family.

Now home, whenever I turn on the car air conditioning, I remember riding in the red pick up truck with the wind and fresh rainwater naturally cooling my face—feeling fully alive and free.

About the Author: Hi, I'm Jordan Solomon from San Francisco. I'm an avid sports fan interested in studying politics/economics in college. I hope you enjoy my essay.

High School Attended: St. Ignatius College Prep, San Francisco, CA

The Process: Lots and lots of brainstorming/drafting/refining. A lot of the essay came from my journal that I kept on my latest trip to Nicaragua.

Acknowledgments: Paula Birnbaum, Neil Solomon

Jordon will be attending Tulane University.

Leadership is a constant theme and emphasis at CMC. One way CMC emphasizes leadership is through the Athenaeum Speaker Series (www.cmc.edu/mmca), which enables CMC students to dine with leaders from a wide range of fields every weeknight during the academic year. Recent speakers have included authors, activists, entrepreneurs, scientists, professors, politicians, and more. If you could invite anyone to speak at the Athenaeum, who would you choose and why? Please limit your response to no more than 300 words.

YITZHAK RABIN:
THE FATHER OF DIALOGUE

Jordon Solomon

"There is no doubt whatsoever in my mind that the risks of peace are preferable by far to the grim certainties that await every nation in war."

–Yitzhak Rabin

"My cousin kills Jews in Israel every day." Nehad told me with a smirk on her face, when I told her I was Jewish. The eight-year-old me was startled and at a loss for words. Your cousins do what? Why did she seem to be bragging about murder? This was my first encounter with the Israeli-Palestinian conflict, but it was not my last.

Eight years later, Michael, a close friend of mine and fellow co-president of our high school's Jewish and Palestinian club, told his family's story to the rest of the Dialogue Club, "My grandparents watched as their home was demolished by wrecking balls. They were left with only the things they could carry on their backs." The Dialogue Club provides a safe place for Jewish and Middle Eastern students to discuss the conflict and share stories. It is an affinity group that represents our particular minorities in the larger context of the Catholic school we both attend. What I've learned most over falafel and shwarma from the dialogues we have cultivated is that once you get to know the "enemy," he or she turns out not to be an enemy at all.

It seemed natural, then, when I had an assignment in world history to research a 20th century leader that I would choose Yitzhak Rabin. I already had a deeply rooted interest in Israeli-Palestinian affairs, and this project challenged me to further explore my interests.

When I first read this essay prompt, I jumped on the opportunity to bring Rabin back from the dead to speak at the Athenaeum. He was the first Israeli leader to recognize the Palestinians as a people, reaching across the table to negotiate with them. In his words, "You don't make peace with friends. You make it with very unsavory enemies." Through the historic agreements made at the Oslo Peace Accords, Rabin made peace with one of his most unsavory enemies, Palestinian leader Yasser Arafat. Tragically, Rabin was assassinated two years after shaking hands with Arafat by a right-wing Israeli extremist who opposed negotiations of any kind with the Palestinians. The morning of his assassination, his wife had reminded him to put on a bulletproof vest, but he refused because he had become so confident that peace was possible. He had come a long way from the violent military commander that he was during the 1948 Arab-Israeli War. Although he only made a small dent in this multi-faceted conflict, Rabin showed the world just how powerful dialogue can be.

And it is dialogue that I would like to open up with Rabin. If he would oblige, I would invite him to my table and ask him the questions that continue to haunt me: "Were you turning in your grave when the wall was built? What do you think of Israeli settlements in Palestinian territory? Do you have any advice on how to interact with Hamas, the terrorist group dictating most of Palestine's politics today? What is your answer to today's conflict?"

I wish, after our talk, I could then teleport him from the Athenaeum at CMC to the negotiating table at the Knesset in Jerusalem. He understood the peacemaking process better than any of the Israeli prime ministers who preceded him, and it would only be right to let him finish the work that he started.

About the Author: One of my goals in life is to facilitate dialogue and bring "enemies" closer together as you will read in this essay.

High School Attended: St. Ignatius College Prep, San Francisco, CA

The Process: As soon as I read the prompt, I remembered writing my sophomore world history paper on Rabin, and thought about what a great essay I could write if I linked his work to my work in the Dialogue Club. The essay started off very history essay-ish at first and resembled my world history paper in some ways. After many drafts, this is the final product I came up with.

Acknowledgments: Paula Birnbaum, Neil Solomon, Gabrielle Glancy.

Jordan will be attending Tulane University.

Some students have a background or story that is so central to their identity that they believe their application would be incomplete without it. If this sounds like you, then please share your story. (Common Application)

MY MIRACLE

Katerin Celeste Spohn

I am a successful senior at Saint Mary's College High School who takes AP English, works on the yearbook staff, and expresses myself creatively in my dance class, which I love. I have lived a miracle.

I am Katerin Celeste Spohn; my name was not always that. I was born in Guatemala where the beach is black and hot at midday that it can give you blisters. My name was Katerin Celeste Chavez Gomez. Life was not easy for a girl born into a family with no education and no annual income. As one of eight siblings, the family cook, and cleaner, my only good memories are when my paternal grandmother would braid my hair, and we would cook together. When she passed away, I was five years old. Her death devastated my father, who turned to drinking, lost his job, and died five months later.

My mother, having five mouths to feed and a job that did not pay enough, returned to her family in the capital but left me with neighbors for about a year. I was physically abused and prayed that my mother would return for me. My only consolation was that I could visit my stepsister who lived a two-hour walk away. Only she showed me love during what I believed to be abandonment by my mother. I was almost seven years old when my mother returned for me. She took me to the capital, where I thought my siblings were, only to find that they were not. She never told me where they had gone. I did not have a chance to say good-bye to them. I was devastated.

My mom took me to the garbage dumps daily to look for food. Although it was expired, the food was a blessing to us. I missed my siblings and asked to visit Monica, my older sister. Out of the blue my mother said, "Vas a ir a visitar a Monica, Katerin." Nothing was explained to me, she packed my things and took me to a stranger named Dina Castro and said goodbye. I thought I would be back, but that was not the case.

I was at a home where kids are sent before meeting their adoptive parents; I did not understand what was happening. I was sitting next to the window, crying as the rain began to fall. It seemed at that moment that the whole world was sad. With my tiny heart ripped apart, and my soul like that of an older woman, I knew that something was not right.

Without realizing, I met my new family, and my sister Monica was there. We moved to Berkeley from Guatemala, but I still did not understand that I had been adopted. To me it was just another trip where I would stay for a while and then my birth mother would come for me. At the age of nine I finally said to my new mom, "When am I going back?" She had not realized that I had wondered for two years when I would see my mother again. She then explained the adoption process, and how I was adopted and could not return to my mother. At that moment I stopped trusting everyone, for in my heart I felt that everyone who loved me would abandon me just like my mother had done not once, but twice.

What in this tragic story is a miracle? The miracle is that I have started trusting again. I am Katerin Celeste Spohn, and this story is central to defining who I am. I am learning with my courage, strength, and determination, with the help of my parents and therapist, to integrate my early life experiences into who I am now and to turn what was devastating to me as a child into personal power. My goal is to become a successful bilingual speech pathologist.

About the Author: I am Katerin Celeste Spohn, I was adopted at the age of seven from Guatemala in 2002 by an American couple. I live in Berkeley, California, with my sister who was adopted with me. My aspirations in life are to become a bilingual speech pathologist and work with kids. I hope to someday have the ability to return to my country.

High School Attended: Saint Mary's College High School, Berkeley, California

The Process: In writing my essay, I had my mother sit and talk with me about my essay prompt. She wrote down my ideas and what I said and gave me the paper so I could have an idea of what I wanted to write about. I wrote out my essay and had about seven people read it in total. My essay went from three pages single spaced to 650 words.

Acknowledgments: I want to thank my mother, teachers, and peers who looked over drafts.

Katerin Celeste Spohn will be attending Western Washington University.

MY LOVE AFFAIR

Mallika Sriram

I like to imagine myself being born with a book in my hand. Amidst the mess and chaos of childbirth, my little head would be the first to emerge, followed by my arms clutching a book, my torso, and my legs, with my feet bringing up the rear. I would have read the book in my mother's womb and gained my understanding of the world that I could not yet experience. Although my eyes enable me to see the world, I find that the best way to understand it is by reading.

I often used to wonder whether it was more important for a book to mirror reality literally or thematically, and I now believe that the latter is far more significant. Life of Pi is a good illustration of this. I was particularly struck by the author's use of allegory to show the difference between humans and animals and the darker aspects of the human psyche. Specifically, the character of Pi/Richard Parker intrigued me. Yann Martel took a convoluted metaphorical idea about the lighter and darker facets of his soul and expressed it simply by splitting the two parts up into entirely separate entities. This instilled in me the idea that people are so complicated that it renders them very difficult to judge fairly. For this reason, I try to avoid, to the best of my ability, being biased about people's personalities. So how then do I understand people?

I also view people in the same way that I examine fictional characters. This enables me to understand both my tangible acquaintances and my fictional ones better and often changes the way in which I see them. If I'm being completely honest, I think that part of my love for my father, which was tested some years ago upon revelations of his infidelity and my parents' subsequent separation, comes from my sense of emotional attachment to Willy Loman, the protagonist of Death of a Salesman. Only by understanding and even appreciating a character whose flaws were glaringly obvious, but whom I still considered not just a sympathetic character but also a good one, did I manage to finally let go of the past and accept my father as a human being, rather than the (now fallen) hero he had once appeared to be.

Literature, books, words—these are all fundamental to my identity. It is through reading that I fall in love with humanity as a whole; it takes a special type of species to appreciate and communicate the beauty and the complexity of existence through the written word. Reading reminds me of our capacity for love, for forgiveness, for empathy. It reminds me that my understanding does not necessarily entail judgment. My love affair with words has made me regard the world with a kinder eye.

About the Author: I've lived in Singapore for the last thirteen years, and I've been reading for as long as I can remember—this, combined with my studying philosophy, psychology, and English, has shaped my world-view and the way in which I understand people. My essay is a reflection of this, detailing the impact that reading has had upon my life. My most cherished dream is to one day write a novel that I can be proud of.

High School Attended: Tanglin Trust School, Singapore

The Process: When I read the list of possible prompts for the Common App long essay, my mind began buzzing with possible responses, and I found that all of them related, in some way or another, to literature. Books and reading have always been a large part of my life, and there are certain books that I keep very close to my heart—I wanted to express this in my essay and connect it to who I am as a person.

Acknowledgments: My school college counselor.

Mallika Sriram will be attending The University of Edinburgh.

Roots

Ayotunde Summers

Dreads are roots. Derived from the biblical story of Samson and Delilah, in my mother's culture, dreadlocks equal power. Like the mane of a lion, they symbolize growth; as the cub grows, so does his mane. My mother, uncles, brothers, aunts, cousins, and grandmother all had the same hair. It unifies us. The only time someone can cut their hair, and it isn't frowned upon, is when they die. The family keeps the hair as a way to honor that person's memory. Strangers identified me as the guy with dreads, but I wanted to be known as Ayotunde Summers, a young man who survived a lot. My hair was heavy and hard to maintain; so was my life.

In eighth grade, my mother had an aneurysm. It was a blessing. Without it, we would never have detected her colon cancer. At that point, I had to get used to the fact that I might not have a mother. At the time, the most basic tasks became a challenge: my room was in disarray, the floor was covered in dirty laundry, the bed was never made, and the prized possessions in my room were completely neglected. Everything in that room had a thin layer of dust, and I did nothing to change that. My hair also received the same level of mistreatment. It remained unwashed, unkempt. This was partly because my mother always did my hair. She was in the hospital, and we all had much bigger concerns; I didn't care what my hair looked like. My mother lost her dreads because of brain surgery. Her life was in danger, and neither she, nor her hair, would ever be the same.

Death is inevitable. I just didn't expect it to be my younger brother to pass away the following year. All members of my family, including myself, cut one of our dreads to connect to him. In return, we took one of his dreads to connect to ours. In theory, we were all connected. My mom was the only one who couldn't participate in this. Technically speaking, neither could my father, but that's because he is bald. I did not want people to know about my situation so, this time, I put in extra time to make sure my hair always looked proper. As a young man who rarely spends lots of time on my appearance, it was something I hated doing—but I did not want pity.

Tenth grade came and welcomed me with a torn ACL. My hair and my body grew out of shape. I needed a distraction from the distractions. It was literally impossible given the fact I could barely move around. It took a lot of rehab hours to get back to form. I needed a change—not just a cosmetic change but rather one with personal meaning: I needed to cut my hair.

The following year I finally did it. A huge weight lifted off my shoulders-literally and emotionally. A new look prompted a much needed drive to try new things. I joined the wrestling team. It turns out that I love it and am pretty good at it, too. Come to think of it, dreads would have been really inconvenient: who wants to wear a giant shower cap when trying to throw a person down to the ground?

I don't miss them at all. Those dreads still remain symbols of family tradition, I realized that, even without them, my roots remain deep, heavy and full of strength.

About the Author: I attend a public high school in New York City and look forward to studying the liberal arts in college as my future career plans are still being weighed. My interests include reading, wrestling, exploring NYC and, of course, girls.

High School Attended: Baruch College Campus High School, New York, NY

The Process: Wow! This was a long journey. I started with a kernel of an idea. I then did a peer review with my English class and they helped me unearth what I was really trying to say. Then I procrastinated for a few weeks and pretended it didn't exist. Then I plunged in. Through writing, and revising, both on my own and with my English teacher, I truly learned a lot about myself—both about my life and about myself as a writer and thinker.

Acknowledgments: my mom, my English class, Ms. Ross

Ayotunde Summers will be attending University of Buffalo.

BERNINI ON THE UNDERGROUND

Caroline Tisdale
— First Prize

There are too many ideas and things and people. Too many directions to go. I was starting to believe the reason it matters to care passionately about something is that it whittles the world down to a more manageable size. —Susan Orleans, *The Orchid Thief*

I am sitting on the Tube, waiting. Above ground, it is night, but below ground it is always the kind of lighting that makes the shadows on one's face green and purple. I am standing on the Tube, by the doors. They open and exhale and inhale masses of people to their respective destinations. We're at Lancaster Gate, three stations away from my stop, and my carriage of the Tube has coughed up most of its passengers. My vision shifts to the left as the Tube slows down and my body can't keep up.

I don't want to see how many people board my car; I don't know if I can stand the magnitude of individual lives and destinations crammed in a long, thin, line dug in the earth. Two stops left. One stop remains, Notting Hill Gate. I start to lift my head. I'll be away from this in a few minutes. I turn to my left. Head fully raised, I find my eyes are locked on one figure sprawled at the head of the tube carriage. I see Bernini's Ecstasy of Saint Theresa, wearing flesh, bleached and paint-stained khakis, and an equally soiled, blue-collared T-shirt. He throws his saintly head back, eyes closed, neck bent in an expression of vulnerability, and mouth open. I look around and check to see if anyone else in the carriage notices him.

My hand slides into my pocket, and feels for a phone. I must capture this moment. I imagine how I would paint him. The background would be red, maybe gold. Everything would fade around his figure, but the outlines of the tube carriage would still exist. The train slides into my station. Holland Park. The need to get out and above seems distant in light of the divine image I found, possessed by a man sleeping off his after-work beers, but the rush of the opening doors remind me of my duty. Finally fingers find the phone in my pocket. I am standing on the platform, alone, at the edge of a photograph. Bernini's man accelerates into the darkness, but his image is emblazoned in my mind.

More people pass me by on the street, on the sidewalk, and on the road. I wonder about the dusty, paint-stained man, and his body being hurdled through a space beneath my feet. What was it about him that conjured up an image in my mind, buried under 350 years of history? What was it about him that made me able to stare at his being, wonder about his existence, and even want to capture it? Why no one else?

It's 12:40-ish, I'm in bed, and I still can't fall asleep. There are thoughts in my mind about the baroque apparition on the underground that evening. I don't want to think of what he's doing now, of how he lives his life outside the state in which I found him, on his westbound commute. I want to keep that moment of illusion alive so it can continue to fuel my thoughts. I reach for my sketchbook and turn on the lights. There's a pen on the floor, and I scribble sketches of sleeping saints. In the morning, I find ink printed on my pillow.

Tomorrow evening I will be sitting on the Tube again, watching the way the fluorescent lights cast shadows like bruises beneath cheekbones and eye sockets. I will stare at the woman sitting across the aisle reading a book and imagine that I created the scuffmarks on her boots with the rough bristles of my paintbrush. I will be sitting, waiting for another apparition.

About the Author: I am an American who has lived abroad, in London, for nine years. My main interest is painting, and I hope to pursue that passion throughout my life, along with my love of writing, reading, and learning.

High School Attended: The American School in London, London, England

The Process: The prompt is "Using a favorite quotation from an essay or book you have read in the last three years as a starting point, tell us about an event or experience that helped you define one of your values or changed how you approach the world." I started off with a quote from a book that features one of my favorite movies, *Adaptation.* The quote describes one's need to find something to be passionate about in order to make all of the information that we intake on a daily basis manageable. I thought of my passion, painting, and how I try to see the world through the lens of an artist waiting for inspiration. This experience on the Tube fit perfectly.

Acknowledgments: I would like to thank my English teacher, Stephan Potchatek.

Caroline Tisdale will be attending Yale University.

ME

Leyla Tonak
– Second Prize

I'm a hipster through and through. I love indie music, infinity scarves, and vegetarian cuisine. And I still believe that art can change the world. But with an anthropologist-turned-public-health-nurse for a mother and a Marxist economist for a father, I have not escaped nerdy academic zeal. I dash back and forth between biology and photography, paintbrush in one hand, French dictionary in the other. Even my childhood was divided, crisscrossing the ocean after my parent's separation.

My sister and I evolved as frog-like tomboys. Amphibious in our pursuits, we would wallow in muddy river beds or cow fields in search of fun. My intrinsic love of nature was nurtured by the hot sun beating down on acres of hay and the soft embrace of snow that wrapped our house in three feet of white. The frigid winters were wood fires and power outages. Summer was pink lemonade. Behind mascara lashes and lacquered nails, there is still a younger me with skinned knees and dirty toes. The rural pastures of my early years are interspersed with bursts of neon color, my travels to the great cities of the world.

I was in elementary school the first time I became aware of the possibility of injustice towards women. Two social workers asked me where I would be uncomfortable with someone touching me. Embarrassed, I pointed. In my father's home country of Turkey, being a woman becomes even harder. Turkey is still a predominantly Muslim nation and many traditionalist politicians still fight to undermine its secular government.

Ever since I can remember, there hasn't been enough money. The trend of young people moving out west for employment has left my hometown economy shriveled. Our high school is sinking into the sewage upon which it was built, dragging our pinhole of opportunity down with it. Our guidance counselor and principal have as much interest in our futures as they have funding for the courses that get cancelled each year. When I decided to apply to college in the States, I knew I would undertake this process on my own. But if there's one thing my community has taught me, it's the value of hard work and perseverance.

Recently, I began volunteering at my local food bank. My first night there was a unique experience. As I hefted bags of flour and jugs of molasses, I watched a myriad of personalities and situations come through the door. With a slow, sinking feeling, I learned just how many people go hungry in my little town. And yet many of them appeared upbeat as they stomped the slush from their boots. Unfortunately, community service is scarce here, and I've had to search for opportunities to volunteer.

I strive for artistic activism. In college, and in life, I wish to address such issues as women's rights, education, poverty, and oppressive religion. But I don't want to do it from behind a desk. I want to do it through the creation of art that is socially relevant and emotionally provocative.

About the Author: I live in Nova Scotia, Canada, with my mother, grandmother and younger sister. I hope to someday use art to change the world.

High School Attended: Annapolis West Education Centre, Annapolis Royal Nova Scotia

The Process: This essay is a patchwork of many different essays I wrote over a period of a few months. Eventually, it came down to selecting the bits that were truest to me and my life and stitching them together.

Acknowledgments: Gabrielle Glancy

Leyla Tonak will be attending Boston University.

FEATHER IN DARKNESS

Leyla Tonak

There came a time when I wasn't sure my feet still hit the ground. I was way up, curled in a storm cloud. All I could hear was the thunder of my sadness. Like a feather in darkness, I floated. My filaments caught nothing but empty space and black. I was adrift in a sea of slow gravity. I have always had a tendency toward dark waters. But gradually this tendency grew to resemble the endless ocean that embraces and imprisons my peninsula home, Nova Scotia. A great, black lake. There is a painting that reminds me of myself, a drowning tree, clawing at the sky. But what I see in this tree is innate, invisible strength. The tree accepts its dark reflection. I was once swallowed up by the murky waters at my feet, and I do not deny those days or their significance. But I lived for the promise of the horizon, that faint and opaque thread that leads beyond this tiny spit of land and its roughly sketched lobster claw outline.

There is a painting of the grey Atlantic, all unmarred sky and silhouettes, which reminds me of home. For years I have watched the sun gilding the tops of the fishing boats. Since my first pair of rubber boots I have been leaving my footprints in the salty muck of the marshes and trekking the billowing yellow hills of the dykes, their brown puddles full of crab shells. I have walked our one wharf, embedded in the wide channel that turns deep blue in the sun. I have seen our steep, green slopes become thick and soggy with color when the leaves turn. I have borne the months of sleet and rivers of melting ice that mix with dirt and make our town look as if it's crying.

I once met a boy with copper hair and caramel eyes. He helped me stay above the surface of the water. I waded, trusting his pale hands to guide me. The waters of the lake turned honey gold in the warmth of his perfect, symmetrical smile. I felt happiness I had forgotten how to feel. The patterns that his freckles made became the cadence of my breaths and the rhythm of my heartbeats.

Then, one day he turned and grasped my hair. He shoved me down, to the depths of the lake where gravity ended. And the lake froze over.

Ms. Delaney was rake thin, with a voice that scratched like sandpaper. Sometimes she would ask me to read to the class when she was tired. She would take me for walks through the snow and cups of hot chocolate with whipped cream. The cancer in her lungs took her from me, and that was the last time a teacher tried to understand me.

There is a painting that reminds me of my father, sharp edges like half-forgotten words. He chose to put nine thousand kilometers between us. And yet, this chasm of damage is not acknowledged. The bright white swirls at the forefront of this piece are his sperm. I confirm his superior genes with each of my accomplishments. My victories cease to be my own. Biology, he says, means that we are eternally bonded. Whatever bonds there might have been, they have no hold on me now.

I have stayed solid by creating. I feel gravity's tender tug when I hold my paintbrushes in my fingers. As paint glides onto canvas, muddy water is extracted from me like poison. I gratefully pour it into my artwork. A kind of silence overtakes me here, in my safest place. Sometimes, I can even bring the paint to life with my body. Dance is being art in every bone. I have learned that art can set you free from pain. And this knowledge has stayed sewn into my skin, through all those water-logged years.

About the Author: I live in Nova Scotia, Canada, with my mother, grandmother and younger sister. I hope to someday use art to change the world.

The Process: This essay was a self-exploration and an exercise in acceptance. I had to be vulnerable and honest in order to truthfully convey who I am and, at the same time, find redemption in my struggles. This essay has been edited to the point where I can say that I am content with every single sentence of it. Nothing is in excess; nothing is omitted. Every piece is necessary and comes straight from my heart.

Leyla Tonak will be attending Boston University.

BREAKING CATHOLICISM

Alexandria Velazquez

After an hour and a half of Sunday school at St. Francis Xavier, my dad was forcing me to attend church with him. With my copy of Harry Potter opened in my lap, I vigorously flipped each page to hear that satisfying sound of paper against paper, waiting patiently for the time to fly by. The pastor's monotonous voice oozed from the loudspeaker and invaded the scene playing in my head. I willed mass to go as fast as possible so I could just be done with religion for the rest of the week until next Sunday. Next Sunday would be the exact same, except maybe I'd bring in a new novel.

My father, a stern Catholic set in tradition, was determined to make his daughter follow in his footsteps. I didn't want to deny him the satisfaction of seeing me pass through all of the Catholic milestones: my first penance, first communion, confirmation. It felt wonderful seeing him beam at me from a pew as he witnessed me, a lanky girl donning a puffy white dress that didn't fit quite right, receiving my first Eucharist. But I realized that this wasn't for me; it was only for him. Not once did I care for reading the word of the Lord, nor did I accept the constricting Catholic ideals summoned during each class at St. Xavier. Never until then did it occur to me that I had a choice.

The day my confirmation came and went, I retired my rosary and Bible into a dimly lit corner. I diligently mulled over my beliefs, giving myself ample time to peruse the corners of my brain. I skipped Sunday masses, cooked breakfasts with my mom, even learned to play the guitar with my newfound time. I realized that I didn't quite know how I felt about God. There was no proof of His existence, yet so many people swore by it. I didn't feel His presence, but millions of other people did. I was at an impasse, so I left it at that, content with at least taking the time and initiative to search within myself. I was completely okay with not knowing how I felt about religion; I felt more pride in that than in accepting something just because it's tradition. It was a year later that I found out the term for this way of thinking: agnosticism. I felt as if, after years of unsuccessfully trying to fit into shoes that pinched and blistered my feet, I'd finally found a pair that fit me perfectly.

My father, however, didn't share my enthusiasm. He instead seemed to be in denial about the entire situation. For a few years he started every Sunday morning off by asking me if I wanted to go to church with him, and every Sunday morning I held my ground, with determination and confidence in my decision to be true to myself. I turned down each of his offers, refusing to let his downtrodden visage sway me into guilt as he walked down the stairs, asking me if I was sure. I responded accordingly, making it crystal clear that I had no regrets about breaking away from Catholicism. I'd finally begun to create my own identity, outlining myself in the most personal ways. I'm continuing to outline myself, daring to close some figures and color them in, whilst still discovering lines that I don't agree with. So I erase those and happily continue outlining.

About the Author: I, Alexandria Evelyn Velazquez, called Alex by pretty much everyone, live in the Bronx and plans to become a doctor of veterinary medicine as well as a part-time guitarist, singer, longboarder, hoopdancer, and horseback rider (and so far I've completed 3/5 of these things).

High School Attended: New Exploration into Science, Technology and Math, New York NY

The Process: I had a really tough time solely deciding whether or not I could properly describe my religious conflict without disrespecting the Catholic religion. I didn't want any admission's faculty who happened to be Catholic to read this and become offended, so I took an incredible amount of care to make my opinions as crystal clear to understand as possible. Besides worrying about possibly offending someone, I actually really enjoyed writing this essay. It gave me the opportunity to not only just go back into the past and recollect a few fuzzy memories, I was also able to clearly find the path that led me to agnosticism.

Acknowledgments: Thanks, Dad, for being the impetus for my religion switch, and thanks, Mom, for helping me keep my sanity throughout the process.

Alexandria Valazquez will be attending NYU College of Arts and Sciences.

ABOUT THE EDITOR, GABRIELLE GLANCY

Former Admissions Director, Series Editor of *Best College Essays*, published in *The New Yorker*, and author of *The Art of the College Essay*, New Vision Learning's Gabrielle Glancy has been in the business of helping students realize their dreams for almost thirty years. With a knack for knowing just the right formula to help high school students succeed where they have struggled and get in where they want to go, she is one of the foremost professionals in her field. Headquartered in the Bay Area, Gabrielle Glancy is well known all around the world for her college admissions expertise.

22202001R00126

Made in the USA
San Bernardino, CA
24 June 2015